Nature at War

Hal Butler

Henry Regnery Company · Chicago

Library of Congress Cataloging in Publication Data

Butler, Hal.
    Nature at war.

    1.   Natural disasters—United States.   I.   Title.
GB5007.B87 1976   973   76-6264
ISBN 0-8092-8141-4

Published simultaneously in Canada by
Beaverbooks
953 Dillingham Road
Pickering, Ontario L1W 1Z7
Canada

Contents

Introduction

This book tells the story of nature at war against mankind. It describes some of the most violent natural upheavals ever to ravage the United States and the Caribbean.

Since the beginning of time, man has been the victim of great natural disasters. He has been drowned, swept away by winds, destroyed by fire, frozen to death, and swallowed up by earthquakes in a sequence of catastrophes that has never ended. But nature alone is not to blame for this tapestry of human tragedy; man's way of life has invited his own destruction.

Man builds his cities and his homes on coastlines subject to hurricanes, on rivers open to flooding, over dangerous faults that spawn earthquakes, in areas ripe for tornadoes, even on the slopes of active volcanoes. Such actions may seem foolhardy, but there are logical reasons for man's incautiousness. The waterways of the world represent avenues of commerce; the land areas vulnerable to nature's whimsicalities are often the best for growing food. Thus the building of man's culture has dictated that he risk his life and his welfare in some of the most dangerous parts of the world.

But there are compensations. A civilization that has laid itself open to the fury of natural forces has also revealed to us the qualities in man that enable him to overcome disaster. No earthquake has ever discouraged him from rebuilding a city on the same shaky ground. No hurricane has prevented him from living in areas where hurricanes are frequent visitors. No flood has convinced man to move from untenable lowlands along the world's rivers. No tornado has deterred him from rebuilding his shattered home where tornadoes are likely to descend again. Nor has any volcanic eruption prevented him from erecting new towns and homes on the slopes where lava has recently flowed.

Whether this deep-seated trait in man denotes supreme courage or reckless abandon, it is certain that man will continue to challenge nature to do its worst—and that nature will respond.

Hal Butler

Earthquake!

Each year about 50,000 earthquakes occur of sufficient size to be detected without the aid of measuring instruments. Man feels them underfoot. Most of these are minor earth tremblings, but at least 100 are large enough to do major damage if they take place near heavily populated areas. This is indeed a shaky planet on which to live.

An earthquake, simply described, is a tremor deep in the earth that creates movement at the surface. All major earthquakes and most of the smaller ones result from strain caused by natural geological processes—the fracture or shifting of underground rocks. A few minor earthquakes, however, are caused by volcanic action or man-made explosions. Some earthquakes come suddenly, with little or no warning; others are preceded by smaller foreshocks; and nearly all of them are followed by aftershocks. When powerful jolts occur successively to cause continuous disturbance, they are referred to as earthquake swarms.

In ancient days many believed that earthquakes were caused by the gods expressing their displeasure with man's ways. Others felt that the earth was mounted on the back of a monstrous animal—a huge catfish, whale, tortoise, frog or spider—and that when the animal moved the earth shuddered. At least those who believed in the monstrous-animal explanation realized one thing—that something underground was causing all the disruption. Today we know what that something is. Rocks deep in the ground are subjected to stresses until they bend or change shape. When the strain exceeds the strength of the rocks, sudden fracture occurs; the rocks break or shift to a new position. This shift is called an elastic rebound. Seismic waves from this rupture radiate to the earth's surface through what are called active geological faults—or, more simply, areas of weakness. The shaking of the ground is produced by these waves.

Earthquakes are caused by disruptions as deep as 450 miles below the surface, but the largest and most destructive quakes usually spring from depths of less than 30 miles.

Here are accounts of the three most destructive earthquakes to occur in the United States.

1

America's Forgotten Earthquake
New Madrid, Missouri (1811)

The greatest earthquake ever to ravage American soil rocked the entire Mississippi Valley at 2 A.M. on December 16, 1811. It began with an angry rumbling deep in the earth's innards, and then the crust rolled in successive undulating waves. Immense fissures, some five miles long, opened in the shuddering earth, and the log-cabin homes of valley settlers toppled out of sight.

The epicenter of the quake—considered one of the three or four most severe earthquakes of all time—was at New Madrid, Missouri, a tiny settlement of 800 people perched precariously on bluffs overlooking the Mississippi River. From this axis the shocks spread out like the spokes of a wagon wheel over an area of one million square miles. Convulsions were felt as far north as Detroit and Canada, as far east as Washington, D.C., as far south as New Orleans, and in Indian encampments 500 miles to the west. The shocks continued for many months, churning the land like a giant mixer, sinking highlands and raising lowlands, creating new lakes and destroying old ones, until the face of the Mississippi Valley was radically changed.

At one point even the mighty Mississippi River bowed to the awesome upheaval by changing course and flowing backward.

Captain Nicholas J. Roosevelt, grand-uncle of Theodore, was proud of his new paddle-wheel steamboat *New Orleans* and optimistic about her chances of making navigational history in the next few months. It was September 28, 1811, and the *New Orleans* was about to embark on a trip from Pittsburgh, down the Ohio River to the Mississippi, and thence to New Orleans. If she made it she would become the first steamboat ever to travel the entire length of the Father of Waters.

In the early part of the nineteenth century the Mississippi River trade was a profitable and growing one, and Captain Roosevelt was anxious to become a part of it. But he had no intention of entering the trade in the usual manner. In those days cargo was carried down the river to the Gulf in inefficient keelboats or flatboats. Arriving keelboats had to be laboriously poled back up the river, and flatboats were broken up in New Orleans and sold for lumber, forcing the crew to return home over the bandit-infested Natchez Trace.

Two years earlier, in 1809, Captain Roosevelt and his bride had made a honeymoon trip to New Orleans on a flatboat, with the bridegroom mixing pleasure and business by warily calculating whether a steamboat could actually navigate the Mississippi. Convinced that it was possible, he persuaded Robert Fulton, who knew a thing or two about steamboats, to build such a vessel for the Mississippi trade.

Over a year and $38,000 later the paddle-wheel steamboat *New Orleans* was finished. She was 116 feet long, with a 20-foot beam, and carried two masts with sails for use in emergency. She had only one deck and her round-bellied hull sat deep in the water.

When the *New Orleans* sailed from Pittsburgh, there was mixed reaction from those who saw her off. Some recognized that the steamboat was about to revolutionize the carrying of cargo to far-away New Orleans. Others predicted that the trip would end in disaster and criticized Roosevelt for taking along his pregnant wife. "If he wants to get himself killed in that golderned contraption, that's one thing," they said. "But he ain't got no right to put his wife and her baby in danger."

Indeed, Mrs. Roosevelt was the only passenger on the *New Orleans*. The crew consisted of Captain Roosevelt, a pilot named Andrew Jack, an engineer, six deckhands, a cook, a waiter, two women servants and a huge Newfoundland dog called Tiger. The journey began uneventfully, with the steamboat clicking off nine miles an hour—a highly acceptable speed in those days. On the second night out, the *New Orleans* docked at Cincinnati to take on coal, and the people of the town gathered to make their own judgment as to whether she would be able to finish her maiden voyage. The consensus of opinion seemed to be that "she might make it down-river but how in tarnation would she ever make it back up?"

Three days later the *New Orleans* reached Louisville, where the Roosevelts were feted at a dinner. Here Roosevelt decided to lay to until local floodwaters deepened the rushing rapids in the channel below Louisville and until Mrs. Roosevelt gave birth to her baby. When both events had occurred, the *New Orleans* "shot the rapids" successfully and on the evening of December 15 docked at Yellow Banks.

Captain Roosevelt, his wife, and the crew retired early, hoping to get a start at dawn. Everyone felt the rest of the trip would be easy now that the so-called Louisville rapids had been passed, and Roosevelt was more certain than ever that the trip to New Orleans would prove the feasibility of steamboat trade on the Mississippi.

Then, at 2 A.M., Roosevelt was awakened by a violent lurch

of the ship. The steamboat rolled from port to starboard and back again several times, almost throwing him from his bed. Alarmed, he struggled into his trousers as his wife's frightened voice came from the darkness.

"What was it?" she asked.

"I don't know. We might have been rammed by a keelboat. I'm going to take a look."

Roosevelt rushed on deck to find several members of the crew, including pilot Andrew Jack, already there. Nobody knew what had happened. They had not been rammed. But they could see that the Ohio River had become uncommonly swollen and was rolling in giant swells. For half an hour they stood at the rail watching the agitated water as the steamboat slowly rocked back and forth. Then, at 2:30, a low ominous rumbling was heard and another jolt was felt. The *New Orleans* rolled violently, tugging at her moorings as if trying to burst free. The men were thrown to the deck, and now there was no longer any doubt in Captain Roosevelt's mind.

"An earthquake!" he said in an awed voice.

It was, indeed.

New Madrid, Missouri, was populated with hard-working frontier families who went to bed early to prepare themselves for the next day's chores. Except for a group of Frenchmen who were dancing away the night at a party, the town was asleep when the earthquake struck.

The people awoke to terror. An unbelievable jolt tossed people from their beds, threw furniture around like toys, toppled chimneys, cracked walls, and collapsed entire log-built homes, burying the owners in debris. Terrified people heard their homes creaking and groaning over their heads, and in the pitch darkness of night they groped their way to doors and fled into open fields. As they ran they felt the once solid earth roll beneath their feet, while trees rocked back and forth as if caught in a violent windstorm.

In the fields incredulous people huddled together on the ground, feeling it tremble as lesser jolts followed the first at short intervals. Although the night was chilly, they dared not return to their homes for fear of being pinned in wreckage. There was nothing they could do but wait for daylight, praying that they would be alive to see it.

But the earthquake did not wait. Half an hour after the first shock, another major shifting of the earth occurred. This jolt was almost as severe as the first, and again the people heard cabins collapsing, the bricks of chimneys rattling to the ground, and felt the earth roll beneath them like a heavy sea.

When dawn came it brought little comfort. A black, sulphurous vapor through which the sun barely penetrated lay over the village, but the residents could see ruined homes, felled trees and strange fissures in the ground. Even the Mississippi River was different. The water level had been on the low side all year, but now the river was a thick, swollen stream with a reddish hue from the mud thrown up to the surface.

The settlers had barely recovered from the shock when, at 7 A.M., another major jolt hit, one that was every bit as violent as the first. Before their eyes they saw more homes clatter to the ground, the river whipped into a muddy foam, and hills and bluffs along the Mississippi crumble and slide into the turgid water. Beneath their feet the ground rose and fell, and trees tilted until their branches interlocked. The billowing waves rolled from the northwest toward the river and the ground rose eight to ten feet at their crest. In many cases the earth split open at the top of the swell, creating deep fissures. From these cracks came a hissing sound, followed by spouts of water mixed with sand that shot as high as the trees. So extensive were the upheavals that entire forests fell in order, like toy soldiers, and gianttrees split in two, half on each side of a fissure.

The words of L. Bringier, a terrified resident of New Madrid, survive in the form of a letter:

> There seemed to be a blowing out of the earth, bringing up coal, wood, sand, etc., accompanied with a roaring and whistling produced by the impetuosity of the air escaping from its confinement, which seemed to increase the horrid disorder of trees being blown up, cracked and split, and falling by thousands at a time. The surface settled, and a black liquid rose to the belly of the horses, which stood motionless, struck with panic. Afterward the whole surface remained covered with holes, which resembled so many craters of volcanoes, surrounded with a ring of carbonized wood, and sand which rose for about seven feet. A few months after, these were sounded and found to exceed 20 feet in depth. . . . A lake was produced 27 miles west of the Mississippi, with trees standing in the water 30 feet deep.

The greatest fear of the settlers was that the earth might swallow them. Noting that the waves creating the fissures ran mostly from northwest to southeast, they began to cut down the tallest trees, felling them crosswise to the great earth-waves. Clinging to the trunks of the fallen trees, the people saved themselves from tumbling into the crevices that opened when the earth rolled.

Some were incapable of such calm reasoning. In the chaos one woman was so terrified that she darted into the woods and ran hysterically until she dropped from exhaustion and died.

The series of quakes played strange tricks. High banks along the Mississippi shoreline caved in, carrying people to their deaths in the river. In one instance a man had a boatload of castings stored in his basement, ready for shipment to New Orleans, when the ground opened and swallowed them in one cosmic gulp. In another incident, a settler living on a neck of land with a small stream near his cabin went to get water from his well and found that the well was no longer there. The stream was now flowing next to his cabin and the well was on the other side.

Many died on the river as the continuous quakes played havoc with the Mississippi. One account described the river's behavior this way:

> At times the waters of the Mississippi were seen to rise up like a wall in the middle of the stream and suddenly rolling back would beat against either bank with terrific force. Boats of a considerable size were often cast high and dry upon the shores. A man who was on the river in a boat at the time of one of the shocks declares that he saw the mighty Mississippi cut in twain, while the waters poured down a vast chasm into the bowels of the earth. A moment more and the chasm filled, but the boat which contained this witness was crushed in the tumultuous efforts of the flood to regain its former level.

John Bradbury, a noted English naturalist, was on a flatboat when the first shock occurred. He reported that he was awakened "by so violent an agitation of the boat that it appeared in danger of upsetting. Immediately the perpendicular banks, both above and below us, began to fall into the river in such vast masses as nearly to sink our boat by the swell they occasioned. The river was covered with foam and drift timber and had risen considerably. Two canoes floated down the river. We considered this as melancholy proof that some of the boats we passed on the preceding day had perished."

In one case a group of flatboats was anchored for the night 40 miles below New Madrid. When the initial shock occurred the boats were smashed together violently, and some of them sank. Crews of the surviving boats, seeing the landslides along the river's shores, put out into the middle of the stream. But as the bottom of the river heaved upward, the surface rose six feet within a minute and rushed forward, carrying the flatboats down-river at terrific speed. Most of them were swamped, their crews drowning in the deadly waters.

In other instances, small boats were swept up small streams that fed into the Mississippi, then left stranded as the waters receded. Numerous boats were smashed to bits against snags and sawyers. One man grabbed the snag that had wrecked his boat and clung to it as waves agitated by successive shocks smashed against him. Half drowned, he was finally rescued by another boat.

Curiously, the earthquake did another man a favor. A Captain Sarpy of St. Louis, along with his family and a considerable amount of money, had tied up at a small island on the evening before the quake. But he was disturbed to find that a party of river pirates occupied a section of the island and, believing that they intended to rob him during the night, he dropped lower down the river. That night the earthquake hit. The next morning Captain Sarpy was amazed to see that the island and its disreputable human cargo had disappeared, dropping to the bottom of the raging Mississippi.

No one slept aboard the steamboat *New Orleans* following the two sharp quakes that had rocked the vessel. Captain Roosevelt was close to despair. He saw his dream of inaugurating steamboat shipping on the Mississippi threatened as lesser quakes occurred at frequent intervals all night. He might endanger his wife and new baby by continuing the journey; yet, it could be safer to travel down the Mississippi than to remain here where the quakes were active. His heart sank as dawn came and the crew looked out over the Ohio River they had yet to traverse before reaching the Father of Waters. During the night much of the shoreline had crumbled, narrowing the channel through which the *New*

Orleans would have to make her way. Fallen trees along the shore added to the problem, and the river itself was a strange murky color and seemed more tumultuous than ever. Captain Roosevelt did not know what decision to make until he was challenged directly by the pilot, Andrew Jack.

"What do we do now?" he asked.

Roosevelt stared at him for a long moment. "We go on," he said finally.

With the hesitancy of a blind man, the *New Orleans* threaded her way down the narrowed channel of the Ohio, avoiding the muddy landslides on either side. All through the day the earth trembled. The crew watched in stunned fascination as bluffs tore away and slid into the river. The weather was hot and sultry, and a murky haze reduced the sun to a glowing copper ball.

When they reached the junction of the Ohio and the Mississippi at Cairo, a strange sight met their eyes. The bottomlands along the river were flooded, and only the upper branches of trees were visible. Paddling among the branches, like children at play, was a band of Indians. When they saw the huge riverboat bearing down on them, some approached to inspect it. Others fled, thinking that the big, white smoke-belching steamboat was a monster disgorged from the inner world by the earthquake.

Andrew Jack made the bend into the Mississippi River with great caution and headed the steamboat south toward New Madrid. He did not know, of course, that New Madrid was the focal point of the great quake that continuously shook the *New Orleans* and stirred the water beneath her. There had always been good dockage at New Madrid, and Jack thought it would be a good place to stay for a few days if things got any worse.

But before they ever reached New Madrid, Jack admitted that he was lost and bewildered.

"I'm not sure where we are," he said. "Everywhere the

channel is altered. Where there used to be deep water, there are now sandbars. Where once there was shallow going, it is now deep. And the shoreline is changed so much that I recognize nothing."

Down through this hell of uncertainty Andrew Jack guided the *New Orleans*. Banks continued to crumble; earthquake waves lashing the ship threatened to ground her; trees were uprooted by the churning earth and fell with mighty splashes into the river. Everyone aboard knew that the steamboat sailed in imminent danger of destruction.

Toward nightfall Jack searched for a place of refuge. Normally, at this point, he used a certain island in mid-stream. But to his surprise he found no island at all. Either he was completely lost or it had sunk beneath the water. The high river bluffs did not seem to be a safe place to dock because they might collapse and bury the boat. Finally, just as it was getting dark, Jack spied a small island and succeeded in casting a line ashore. He moored the steamboat to a large tree and, for the first time that day, breathed a sigh of relief.

No one slept that night. The crew spent most of its time on deck, alert to any possible emergency. They could see little of what was going on around them, but the noises of the night were terrifying. Continuous shocks caused landslides that roared like thunder as earth crumbled and splashed into the river. The steamboat was jolted viciously and waves drenched her deck. In her cabin, Mrs. Roosevelt tried to quiet her baby as the room rocked and furniture and loose articles tumbled about her.

At dawn the sight that met their eyes was wildly incredible. Everything around them had changed. The high banks they had avoided had disappeared; a stretch of lowlands had risen six feet; the water was spotted with giant whirlpools; and, most amazing of all, the island to which they had been moored was gone!

"We must have broken loose and drifted," Jack said.

"I don't think so," Roosevelt replied, pointing to the

mooring line. It was still stretched over the bow, but now it went straight down. The rope was still attached to the tree, which had been engulfed with the island!

The deckhands cut the steamboat loose and the ship proceeded down the Mississippi. Under Jack's skilled hands, the *New Orleans* fought the angry river. She managed to avoid the powerful whirlpools that could conceivably sink her. She changed speed when necessary and dodged drifting tree trunks and other navigational hazards. It was then that Roosevelt realized what steam was doing for them. Where flatboats, keelboats and other small craft were sucked down into the river's depths by whirlpools or thrown ashore, steam gave the *New Orleans* the power to withstand or avoid such disasters.

Roosevelt reasoned that if he could get to New Orleans under conditions like these, then no one could ever doubt that steam was indeed the answer to safe navigation on the Mississippi.

As the riverboat neared New Madrid, Jack said, "I think we ought to put in here and stay until all this ends."

Roosevelt looked dubious. He didn't like the idea of giving in to the forces of nature, however violent, but he supposed there was wisdom in Jack's suggestion.

"Very well," he said, "let's put in for a day or two."

As it happened, they did not stay long at New Madrid. The village was in chaos, its citizens overcome by terror. Houses and stores had collapsed. The village was laced with wide fissures, into which some of the houses had tumbled. Many of the inhabitants had already fled to higher ground, but others moved through the streets as if in a daze, some searching aimlessly among the wreckage of their cabins. Landslides were still occurring near the river; part of the city had risen as underground pressures built up; another section had sunk several feet. Great crevices emitted steam and sometimes water, and the very ground hissed and groaned like some unearthly, mortally wounded beast.

The people who had been staring in awe at the big steamboat suddenly decided that it might provide a way to safety for them. They rushed to the dock and begged Captain Roosevelt to take them aboard, but there were so many of them that the captain dared not do so.

As Roosevelt and the crew looked with sinking hearts at the damaged town and its terrorized populace, the earth gave a great, convulsive shudder. The cemetery on a small bank along the river suddenly crumbled, and earth, bodies, coffins, and headstones cascaded into the Mississippi.

From the appearance of the devastated town, Roosevelt guessed that they had arrived at the focal point of the earthquake. He had traversed enough of the quake-torn Ohio and Mississippi rivers by this time to know that the earthshakings were surprisingly widespread. But he could never have imagined the true geographical extent or the amazing nature of the damage levied. For 300 miles along the Mississippi and well up the Ohio, the country was convulsed. Vast regions of the Mississippi Valley had been reduced to a wasteland, covered with sand and split by steaming fissures. In some of the giant cracks, rushing water from nearby swamps had created streams; narrow rivers had left their beds and made new channels through the cracks. In one place a district of 30,000 square miles had sunk from five to 25 feet; other areas had been similarly raised.

Entire forests were denuded, cattle destroyed, and many people killed. In some cases the bottoms of lakes heaved upward, spilling water into lowlands to form new lakes. In the northwest corner of Tennessee a mighty convulsion occurred when forests and canebrakes sank as much as 25 feet. Into this depression the waters of the Mississippi seeped, forming Reelfoot Lake, 25 miles long, five miles wide and 25 feet deep.

The severest earth disturbances occurred in an area of some 50,000 square miles. In this section there were outcroppings of land that looked like domes, sunken areas, fissures, sinks, sand blows and monstrous landslides. Fanning out from this central area was another immense section that suffered lesser earth convulsions, such as the crumbling of smaller bluffs and the uneasy rolling of the land. And on the outer edge there were light tremors that toppled chimneys, downed fences and shattered dishes and windows. The vast area affected included settlements on the Red and Washita rivers 500 miles southwest of New Madrid; the Gulf Coast 500 miles to the south; the nation's capital 700 miles to the east; Boston, 1,100 miles distant; and the "upper reaches" of Canada. Altogether the shocks were pronounced in an area of more than one million square miles, or *half of the entire United States.*

When the cemetery at New Madrid slid into the Mississippi River, Captain Roosevelt decided that it was time to leave. The big paddle-wheel churned the muddy waters into a brown froth and the *New Orleans* moved warily to the middle of the river. He was right to be cautious. The crew members were to face one more fantastic threat to their lives, more violent than any they had yet experienced.

Just south of New Madrid as the *New Orleans* proceeded carefully downriver, Jack cried out in alarm. Roosevelt and the pilot could not believe their eyes. A mountain of earth had risen up before them, spanning the entire width of the Mississippi. From this huge formation the waters of the river cascaded down, sending a ten-foot high tidal wave in their direction.

"My God, we'll be swamped!" Jack shouted.

There was nothing they could do to avoid a head-on collision with the waters rushing toward them. The crew grabbed at anything firm that would keep them from being washed overboard, and then the mountainous wave hit. For a moment the world was nothing but muddy water, and the force of the tidal wave rocked the riverboat until Roosevelt feared the vessel would be crushed. But, miraculously, the *New Orleans* remained intact—as the raging torrent of mud and water that was now the Mississippi *flowed backward.*

For three hours, after the first hideous onslaught, the earthquake-tide rushed upstream at frightening velocity. The great torrent overflowed the banks and flooded the countryside for miles around. It overturned small boats and hurled them inland for more than a mile, and others—caught in great whirlpools—went to the bottom.

Against the weird reversal of the Mississippi, the *New Orleans* could make no progress. She needed all the steam power she could muster just to stay even and not be swept back to the mouth of the Ohio, until at last the Mississippi returned to normal and renewed its natural flow.

As the *New Orleans* picked its way southward, the earth-shocks grew fewer in number and the land along the shore looked more normal. When the steamboat finally moored at Natchez, where the major damage from the quakes were toppled chimneys and cracked plaster, Roosevelt knew they had survived the worst of it. He stepped ashore, got down on his knees, and thanked God for deliverance.

At Natchez, the *New Orleans* picked up a shipment of cotton—the first freight ever carried by a Mississippi steamboat. Five days later, on January 12, 1812, the intrepid riverboat landed safely at New Orleans.

Captain Roosevelt could not have chosen a better time (or a worse time, depending on how one looks at it) to prove that steamboat travel on the Mississippi was possible. The *New Orleans* had run the gauntlet of nature's anger and become the first steamboat to negotiate the Father of Waters.

Although the *New Orleans* was now safe, the terrible earthquake was not over. Shocks continued to radiate outward from New Madrid. Hard jolts occurred on January 23, February 4, 5 and 7—and over the next three months 1,874 shocks were recorded, many of them rated severe. Eventually the violence tapered off, but jolts continued for more than a year and minor agitation was felt for two years. During that long period the Mississippi Valley continued to be the epicenter, but shocks were felt in such cities as Richmond, Virginia; Louisville and Frankfort, Kentucky; Chillicothe, Ohio; Detroit, Pittsburgh, and even New York City. The New Madrid earthquake stands today as one of the few instances where such prolonged shaking occurred in a region remote from any volcanic action.

During these frightening two years many settlers were granted new lands by the government in safer areas, thus seriously delaying development of the Mississippi Valley. But at last the rains beat the sand into the earth and the fissures closed. New settlers came into the valley to clear farmlands— and the greatest quakes ever to strike the American continent were only dimly remembered.

Many steamboats—better designed and better powered— followed the *New Orleans* down the Mississippi. But the *New Orleans'* epic journey, under the most difficult conditions imaginable, had shown them the way.

What eventually happened to the courageous *New Orleans?* Shortly after completing her hazardous first trip, she began a weekly shuttle service, carrying both passengers and freight, between New Orleans and Natchez. In 1815 she carried troops from Natchez to New Orleans to bolster Andrew Jackson's defense of that city against the British in the Battle of New Orleans. Then, six months later, the valiant steamboat that had weathered the greatest natural calamity in American history came to an ironic end. Docked at Baton Rouge, she was impaled on a stump when a drop in river depth occurred, and sank to the bottom—ending one of the strangest riverboat sagas of all time.

2

Disaster on the Bay
San Francisco (1906)

Along the coastline of California, stretching for hundreds of miles, lies a geologically ancient rift in the earth's crust known as the San Andreas Fault. It is the greatest such fracture on earth, and it poses a constant and gnawing danger to the heavily populated cities of San Francisco and Los Angeles as well as to the many coastal and inland towns that dot the map of the Golden State

The movement and shifting of this fault has caused most of California's past earthquakes. At frequent intervals through the years earth shocks—some mild, some severe—have rumbled across the land, and records show that long-forgotten major jolts of the earth's surface occurred in 1864, 1898 and 1900. But none was so violently destructive as the great San Francisco Earthquake of 1906—a giant slippage of a segment of the San Andreas Fault that shook an area 270 miles in length and spread for 40 miles inland and for unknown distances out to sea. Unfortunately, the epicenter of this terrible earthquake was directly beneath the booming city by the bay, and San Francisco became the first—and, to this time, the only—major U.S. city ever to be destroyed by an earthquake.

It was early morning. Enrico Caruso, the famous Italian operatic tenor, was asleep in his ornate suite in San Francisco's elegant Palace Hotel. He was sleeping the sleep of a contented man. The previous evening he had given a memorable performance as Don José in Georges Bizet's *Carmen* before 3,000 people in San Francisco's Grand Opera House. He had sung the role with such skill that the audience had honored him with a standing ovation and he had been forced to make a countless number of curtain calls. Afterward he had put a final touch to a magnificent evening by dining at a famous restaurant, where his fellow performers had toasted him with champagne.

Caruso was happy to be in San Francisco. In fact, he felt that he owed to none other than the Supreme Being a vote of thanks for guiding him to the city on the bay. He had left Naples for the United States just prior to an eruption of Mount Vesuvius, and he was convinced that God had removed him from the danger zone to save his voice and provide him the opportunity to add luster to his already famous name. Feeling safe, secure, and enormously satisfied, Caruso had gone to bed with the knowledge that he was an important person whom the Good Lord was determined to protect.

Then, suddenly, his security was shattered. A tremendous jolt almost threw him from his bed. His eyes popped and his scalp tingled with sudden fright. To his amazement he saw the room rocking like a storm-tossed ship. Pictures had fallen from the walls; plaster was cascading from a cracked ceiling, sprinkling him with a white powder; his bureau drawers were scattered about the room. Still half asleep, he was not sure what had happened, but the abnormality of the situation convinced him of the danger. Sitting bolt upright in his bed he tried to cry out, but his throat was dry and only a croaking noise emerged. His face paled. A sense of outrage gripped him. God had deserted him! The Supreme Being had destroyed his voice! He sobbed.

Meanwhile, a few blocks away from the Palace Hotel, another performer slumbered peacefully. He was 24-year-old John Barrymore—not as well-known as Caruso but a comer in show business—who was soon to leave for Australia to appear in several plays. Just where Barrymore was sleeping when the quake hit is a subject of dispute. It is known that he had attended the performance of *Carmen* the evening before the earthquake, and one story has it that he met a young man who had a collection of fine Chinese porcelain and that he had gone to the man's apartment to see it. There he had spent the night sleeping on a couch. Another story insists that young Barrymore met a delectable young lady at the opera that evening, had taken her out afterward, and had spent the night in her apartment.

In any case, Barrymore was awakened by the same earth-shudder and, taking it much more calmly than Caruso, he slowly dressed in his evening attire and ventured forth to view the damage.

There were other famous people in San Francisco on the morning of the earthquake—Jack London, novelist; Olive Fremstad, who played the title role opposite Caruso in *Carmen;* author Mary Austin; and, just north of the city in Sebastopol, Luther Burbank, the horticulturist—and soon the San Francisco they had known the night before would lay in ruins.

Such a fate seemed untimely, for San Francisco—perilously situated on a peninsula, with the Pacific Ocean on the west and San Francisco Bay on the east—was a growing and prosperous city of some 400,000 people. Its residents were acutely aware that the city had everything it needed to guarantee a great future and would, in time, become one of the great metropolises of the world, rivaling New York, London and Paris. There was money in the town, visible in the elegant mansions of the wealthy on Nob Hill; there were plenty of laborers living in the squalid tenements south of Market Street to do the city's work; industry was growing rapidly; and the town was becoming an important seaport. San Francisco was poised on the edge of greatness, ready to take its place as the focal point of the entire West Coast.

Then, at 5:12 A.M. on Wednesday, April 18, 1906, San Francisco's dream of greatness was shaken by the most destructive earthquake ever to strike an American city. The sudden attack was savage. Houses toppled, chimneys collapsed, huge businesses crumbled, ugly fissures opened in the street—all in a matter of minutes.

The northern portion of the San Andreas Fault had slipped its moorings, and the result was unimaginable destruction. The quake that reduced San Francisco to rubble was felt all the way from Los Angeles to Coos Bay, Oregon. Its power splintered giant redwood trees, tore up highways, demolished houses and barns, and churned the ground into porridge. Before it was over it had changed the face of much of California, sinking land in some places and elevating it in others.

In the process town after town was shattered. The business section of San Jose fell in a heap. Every brick building in Santa Rosa crumbled. At Agnews an insane asylum caved in and buried 100 inmates, the rest escaping to roam the countryside. Northeast of San Francisco, in Solano County, a mile of railroad track sank from three to six feet. Stanford University's relatively new campus suffered major damage.

Many people huddled in their homes, listening to creaking timbers and fearing they would be buried alive under debris. Others ventured into the streets only to be killed by falling bricks from buildings. Chaos reigned everywhere.

But one man remained calm, and his account of the earthquake became one of the most accurate analyses to emerge from the tragedy. He was Professor George Davidson of the University of California in Oakland, who had formerly worked for the United States Geodetic Survey. He was jarred from his bed by the early-morning quake and, as the shock waves rolled beneath his feet, he carefully recorded for posterity the sequence of the earth's shudders. Later he explained how he did it:

> The earthquake [he said] came from north to south and the only description I am able to give of its effect is that it seemed like a terrier shaking a rat. I was in bed, but was awakened at the first shock. I began to count the seconds as I went toward the table where my watch was, being able through my practice closely to approximate the time in that manner. The shock came at 5:12 o'clock. The first sixty seconds was the most severe. From that time on it decreased gradually for about thirty seconds.
>
> There was then the slightest perceptible lull. Then the shock continued for about sixty seconds longer, being slighter in degree this time. There were two more slight shocks afterward, which I did not time. Then at 5:14 I recorded a shock of five seconds duration and one at 5:15 of two seconds. There were slight shocks at 5:17 and 5:27. At 6:50 there was a sharp shock of several seconds.

Author Mary Austin described her experience with fewer statistics and more embellishment. "I wakened sharply to see my bureau lunging solemnly at me across the width of the room. It got up first on one caster and then on another like a table at a seance and wagged its top portentously." Then she looked outside. "I saw a rose tree and a palm tree replacing one another as in a moving picture. I recall the red flare of a potted geranium undisturbed on a window ledge in a wall of which the brickwork dropped outward while the roof had gone through the flooring; and the cross-section of a lodging house parted cleanly with all the little rooms unaltered, and the halls like burrows, as if it were the home of some superior sort of insect laid open to the microscope."

Meantime, Enrico Caruso was neither as calm as Professor Davidson nor as observant as Mary Austin. Instead, he was displaying such histrionics that, had he been on stage, he would have surely earned himself another standing ovation. His only audience, however, was Alfred Hertz, conductor of the orchestra at the Grand Opera House, who rushed into the singer's room to see if he was hurt.

"We are doomed!" Caruso croaked.

"It was an earthquake," said Hertz. "It's over now. Are you injured?"

"My voice!" Caruso said huskily. "The shock has ruined my vocal cords."

"Nonsense. Come to the window."

Caruso left his bed, stumbled to the window, and looked out. All was confusion below. Men and women, still attired in night garments, ran aimlessly or stood dumbstruck in the streets. The fronts of buildings across the street had fallen off, exposing the interiors.

"Sing!" Hertz demanded.

"What?"

"Sing! Test your voice."

Caruso hesitated. Then he burst forth with powerful tones. The people in the street looked up, some even smiled, somehow soothed by the great tenor's voice.

Later Caruso described his adventures in quick, breathless sentences. "I waked up," he said, "feeling my bed rocking as though I am on a ship. From the window I see buildings shaking, big pieces of masonry falling. I hear the screams of men and women and children. The ceiling plaster fell in a great shower. I run into the street. All day I wander about. I try to get away, but soldiers will not let me pass. That night I sleep on the hard ground. My legs ache yet from so rough a bed.''

Actually, Caruso did not suffer unduly. The day after the quake the Metropolitan Opera troupe hired a wagon and driver for $300 to take them and their luggage to the ferry to Oakland. But it is rumored that as the ferry departed Caruso, angry at having been exposed to such danger, shook his fist at the battered city of San Francisco and vowed never to return.

John Barrymore, less ruffled, walked the city for five hours in his opera cape, an impeccable dandy stepping daintily through the rubble. Late in the day he sent a wire to his sister, Ethel, in New York. It explained that he had wandered for hours in a semi-daze and had finally been conscripted by soldiers, who gave him a shovel and ordered him to help clear the streets. When Ethel received the message she showed it to her uncle, John Drew, asking him if he believed it. Drew had never been enchanted by young Barrymore's efforts to become an actor, and he made a remark that has lived in memory.

"I certainly do believe it," he said. "It *would* take an act of God to get John out of bed and the U. S. Army to put him to work!''

Luther Burbank, in Sebastopol, was awakened when his bed began to tremble. He didn't panic. He had been through more than 100 earthquakes in his time and they were to him mere annoyances. However, he was concerned about his garden. Getting out of bed, he staggered over a moving floor and out into the yard to inspect his beloved plants. He found that the quake had moved them out of position—replanting them, so to speak—but that they had not been damaged. Satisfied, he calmly returned to his house.

One man—the only person who had a detailed plan to save the city in event of a great fire—was felled almost immediately. He was Fire Chief Dennis Sullivan, who had just returned to the Bush Street firehouse after fighting an all-night blaze at the California Cannery Company warehouse. Exhausted, he had gone to bed in his room on the third floor of the firehouse only a couple of hours before the earthquake struck.

When the sudden quake rocked his room, Sullivan leaped from his bed. His greatest concern was for his wife, who was sleeping in a bedroom down the hall. He dashed down the corridor to rescue her, but he never reached his destination. The California Hotel, next door to the firehouse, swayed crazily as the earth rumbled beneath it. With a roar it collapsed, dropping a heavy slab of its cornice through the firehouse roof. The structure crumbled under the impact and Sullivan was pinned in the wreckage. His wife was unhurt, but Sullivan died a few days later.

San Francisco was shaken four ways by the monster quake. Following an ominous rumble—familiar to many Californians who had experienced previous earthquakes—the city shuddered under a horizontal shifting of the San Andreas Fault, a dislocation that caused the earth beneath the city to roll like the sea. Almost immediately a vertical movement also made itself felt, causing the city to reel under the violence of both up-and-down and back-and-forth attacks.

Buildings all over the city began to crumble. The City Hall, a modern $7,000,000 structure, collapsed. The Hall of Justice and the jail were severely damaged. A printing plant caved in, the heavy presses crashing through weakened floors. People rushing from buildings were killed as falling bricks and cornices struck them down. A few tall, steel-framed buildings swayed like reeds but stood up under the onslaught, looming among the ruins like soldiers standing guard.

Chimneys toppled or were thrown from roofs all across the heaving city. Streetcar tracks were uprooted and bent into surrealistic shapes. Underground water pipes split open and water fountained to the surface and ran like uncontrolled rivers down the streets.

East of Market Street, in the slums along Howard, decrepit hotels and flophouses were flattened, killing dozens of indigents. West of Market Street, the sloping area known as Chinatown was leveled. On the bay, Long Wharf disintegrated, and thousands of tons of coal slid into the waters. The wholesale district was hard-hit, with men, horses, wagons and bricks from crumbling walls mixed together in an unbelievable heap. Fortunately the quake had struck at 5:12 in the morning, before factory and dock workers had arrived at their jobs and children at their schools. This fact alone kept the death toll from mounting astronomically.

As if the shaking of the city were not enough of a tragedy, the epic seismic disturbance also sparked one of the worst urban fires in history. Before it was contained, the holocaust destroyed the greater part of San Francisco—a mammoth circle 25 miles in circumference that included the business district, the industrial area and many residential sections.

The fire proved virtually unstoppable. Had it begun in one place and swept through the city, firefighters might have had a chance to halt it somewhere along the line. Instead, it sprang up in a thousand different places at once. (Later there was controversy among experts as to whether Fire Chief Sullivan's plan for fighting a city fire would have been effective. Some claimed that it would have stemmed the conflagration; others maintained that it would have been useless since it did not make allowance for simultaneous, widely scattered fires.)

The pattern of the fires resulted from the widespread disruption caused by the quake. Gasoline stoves and lamps were upset, starting blazes in homes. Chimneys were ruptured, scattering hot ashes. Gas mains were wrecked. Furnaces were overturned and industrial chemicals splashed about. Boiler rooms in factories were demolished, causing the boilers to burst. Downed trolley wires lay in the streets, spitting dangerous sparks. And then the gas works near Market Street blew up and added a major inferno to the scene.

The San Francisco Fire Department struggled mightily but with little success. Within minutes after the quake hit, firefighters received sixteen calls. Equipment was rushed from one emergency to another, but it was impossible to quench every blaze. Some fires in private homes were extinguished, but many dwellings burned to the ground before firemen could reach them.

In the wholesale and factory districts the fire raged. Chemicals and stored material in the buildings fed the blaze and the flames spread uncontrollably. To add to the firemen's woes, the earthquake had broken water mains and there was little or no water.

Within three hours the many small fires had merged into nine distinct major blazes that roared through the stricken city. The wind, slight but steady, spread the holocaust. Freight sheds, oil tanks, factories, lumber yards, warehouses, retail stores and jerry-built homes went up in smoke and flame. The heat was so intense that buildings burning on one side of a street ignited those on the other side by spontaneous combustion.

All through the city the frightened people fled, threading their way between burning buildings, stumbling over debris, battling to get away from the fiery death that pursued them. Some of them pushed or pulled wheelbarrows, baby carriages and wagons filled with their most precious belongings. Others carried treasured pictures or delicate vases. One woman fled with a canary in a cage; another lugged a heavy mantel clock. Some carried infants in arms; others dogs and cats. One couple pushed a sewing machine down the street.

There were even comic touches. One impeccable fellow, with his neighbors' houses burning around him, took time to shave and comb his hair. Then he calmly dressed, packed a bag, and strolled from his home. It was not until he was in the street that he noticed he had forgotten to put on his pants.

South of Market Street, the crowded district of the poor was destroyed within hours. The Palace Hotel, where Caruso had stayed, was gutted. The Call Newspaper Building, a half-block away, became a giant torch.

Throughout the long day a great exodus from the city took place. Many people, seeking open ground, fled toward the sanctuary of Golden Gate Park. Others, hoping to board ferries that would take them across the bay to Oakland, headed for the waterfront. Fortune smiled on them, for it was in the bay area that firefighters enjoyed one small victory. Using fireboats to spray the shoreline with salt water from the bay, firemen were able to save most of the wharves and docks. Ferries, barges and tugboats darted about transporting refugees from the burning city.

Meantime, city officials sought to stem the panic. Eugene E. Schmitz—a veteran of the Yukon gold rush, as well as a talented violinist who had risen from the Musicians Union to the mayor's chair—wired other communities for help, conscripted able-bodied men for fire-fighting and rescue work, and sent horses and wagons to powder houses in outlying areas with orders to bring all the dynamite available in the event that it became necessary to blow up buildings to stop the fire. General Frederick A. Funston, in command of what was then called the California Department of the Army, sent soldiers into the stricken areas to battle blazes, organize hospital and first-aid units in the rubble of the streets, form rescue parties, and guard against looters.

But despite heroic efforts, the great fire raged all day long and through the night. The next day it leaped across Market Street to seek more victims in the business, hotel and amusement districts. A fast-traveling fire quickly incinerated what was left of Chinatown. The notorious Barbary Coast went up in flames as lurid as its reputation for sin, vice and wickedness. A group of Italians living on Telegraph Hill used casks of precious wine to soak rags and put out embers that fell on their roofs. On Nob Hill the wealthy set made hasty preparations to abandon their glittering mansions and flee for their lives.

Victims pinned under debris posed a major problem to rescue workers. Men labored frantically to free them before they were engulfed by fire. One man, pinned down by wreckage, watched as flames crept closer and closer, aware that the dozen men who worked to free him labored in vain.

"Shoot me!" the man cried. "I don't want to be burned to death. Shoot me!"

But the rescuers worked until their own hands and faces were scorched. Then, realizing that the situation was indeed hopeless, one of them drew a pistol from his belt and shot the man.

In another case, three priests from St. Patrick's Church granted the last rites to five men who had been dragged from the ruins of a collapsed building. A large piece of coping overhead threatened to fall and crush them all, but not until the ceremony was completed did the five men and the priests escape to a safer place. Three of the injured men died later.

O. M. Nichols, a New Yorker visiting San Francisco, told of his attempt to leave the city for Oakland. "Reaching the bay, we found there was no ferry," he related. "An old fellow had a tugboat tied up. There were several of us wanting to go to Oakland. We asked the boatman what he would take to land us there. He said $250. We chipped in $50 apiece and took the tug."

George Musgrove, a theater manager from Australia, had more difficulty:

> I shall never [he said] forget the scene at the ferry house. It was bedlam, pandemonium and hell rolled into one big pile. There must have been 10,000 persons trying to get on a boat.

Men and women fought like wildcats to push their way aboard. Clothes were torn from the backs of both men, women and children indiscriminately. Women fainted and there was no water at hand to revive them.

Men lost their reason at those awful moments. One big, strong man beat his head against one of the iron pillars on the dock and cried out in a loud voice, "This fire must be put out! The city must be saved!"

When the gates were opened to the boat the mad rush began. All were swept aboard in an irresistible tide. We were jammed on the deck like sardines in a box. No one cared. We were out of the smoke-filled atmosphere and were on our way to a place of comparative safety.

Almost everyone thought the end of the world was at hand. Native sons of San Francisco had experienced earthquakes before. But this was something worse. They had no communication with the outside world. Naturally they imagined that the disturbances were being repeated all over the country.

This observation had much truth to it. Wild rumors spread rapidly through the city—it was a world-wide disaster; Chicago had slipped into Lake Michigan; New York City had been inundated by a huge tidal wave; fire had destroyed both London and Paris. Gruesome stories caught the peoples' imaginations—the quake had wrecked the zoo, freeing wild animals who were now feeding on people who had fled to Golden Gate Park; the quake had churned up bodies in the cemeteries, scattering decaying corpses among those seeking safety nearby. None of these rumors was true, but they added a macabre touch to the occasion.

Miss Martha Sibbels escaped from the shaking Randolph Hotel and ran into the street.

> Someone passing us [she said] advised us to get to as high ground as possible. We started walking as fast as possible to the high parks back of the city. Fire was starting in hundreds of places over the city and the streets were crowded with hurrying refugees.

Where people were unable to procure horses, men and women had harnessed themselves to carriages and were drawing their belongings over the streets. In the residential districts where wealthy people lived we saw automobiles drawn up and loaded down before houses. The owners remained until the flames came too near, and then they got into their machines and made for the hills. We saw one man pay $2,000 for an automobile in which to take his family to a place of safety.

Before night we reached high ground away from the flames. People half-clothed, unfed, hysterical, searching for loved ones, crowded the ground. We passed the night sleepless with a panic-stricken multitude.

In the morning we started toward the harbor with the assistance of soldiers from the Presidio, who had already been on duty twenty-four hours. We got to the wharf and sought to get a launch to Oakland. We were unable to do so, but we were kindly treated by an old skipper who was himself in deep grief because his brother had been crushed to death in their little house. He gave us coffee, the only nourishment we had had except for a few crackers in twenty-four hours.

Then the skipper saw the Government boat cruising in the bay, and said if we could reach the Presidio wharf we could escape on the Government boat. We therefore hurried toward the Presidio, greatly impeded by fissures which stretched long distances and around which we had to make our way. At the Presidio we were taken aboard with other refugees, and a short time later we were safe in Oakland.

Mr. C. C. Kendall, of Omaha, described his attempt to escape the burning city in this way:

I climbed over dead bodies, picked my way around flaming debris, and went over almost insurmountable obstacles to get out of San Francisco. The debris was piled up along Market Street. Fires were raging in every direction. Market Street had sunk at least four feet. It is only a few blocks from the Palace to the ferry, but it took me from six A.M. to 10:15 A.M. to cover the distance.

Men and women fought each other at the entrance to the

ferry like infuriated animals. As the boat pulled out over the bay the smoke and flame in the city rose sky-high, and the roar of falling buildings and the cries of the people filled the air.

Children suffered too. Mrs. Henry Huskey, a resident, described the plight of the children best:

> Under our own observation [she said] was the case of a child ill with diphtheria who was carried into the streets Wednesday night by her parents and died in agony on a lawn the next morning. Utter lack of water in some districts got the children moaning and pleading for a drink. Men of ruined families made every effort to satisfy the thirst of their little ones. At last, in desperation, they invaded the neighborhood saloons and brought whiskey to the women.
>
> Unable longer to withstand the pleading of their children, mothers poured small quantities of the fiery liquor into tin cans and other receptacles and gave it to the tots to drink. The natural result was to increase the pangs of thirst twentyfold, and the sight of woebegone, staggering children was witnessed.

One man experienced in both earthquakes and fires was Dr. Frank A. Brewster, visiting from New York:

> I witnessed the burning of Chicago in 1871 and was in Charleston when an earthquake wreaked destruction there [he said] but the San Francisco horror far outshadows those calamities. I cannot believe the loss of life in San Francisco was confined to mere hundreds. I would be the last to stretch the facts, but I am convinced several thousand persons suffered death.
>
> Thieves and ghouls were dealt with summarily. I witnessed the demise of several ghoulish men. I saw a fellow cutting rings from the hands of a dead woman. There was a rush of men and within a few minutes the robber was dangling from a pole.
>
> One innocent man met his death at the hands of the military. He was a cashier of a bank and refused to obey a command to halt, but continued to run into the bank building. He was shot.

Some people used the tragedy to make money. Arthur

Woodson, a Chicagoan, was staying at the Pacific Hotel at the time the earthquake struck:

> After breakfast [he said] I hustled around to get over the bay to Oakland. A few hacks were in commission and a regular auction was held over the seats sold to each passenger. The prices ranged from $20 to $100. I got a seat in one of the hacks for $35. There were three other men in it that paid $50 for seats.
>
> We had to go to the ferry in a roundabout way, and when we had covered several blocks two men halted the driver. They offered him $300 apiece for the privilege of riding to the ferry. The driver took one up on the box with him, handed me my $35, and made me get out so that the other $300 passenger could get into the carriage.
>
> I hailed the next hack that came along and got up on the box with the driver. Another fellow from the sidewalk called out that he would give $75 to be taken to the ferry, but I told the hack driver that I would throw him off the box if he stopped, as he had no room, inside or out, for another passenger.

J. H. Fiske, another man from Chicago, was sleeping in a room on the third floor of the Terminus Hotel when the quake hit. He started down the stairs but they crumbled beneath him and he fell into the lobby.

"I have not a scar to show for the fall of two stories," he said, "but a few bruises make my body sore and tender. I guess I have my lucky stars to thank that I came through the Johnstown flood, the Galveston hurricane, and the San Francisco earthquake without injury."

During the second night of the fire, the flames swept toward the western section of town. They played no favorites, wiping out the simple wooden residences on the western slopes of the city and the wealthy mansions on Nob Hill alike. But one large residential section in the western part of town remained untouched, and firefighters saw a chance to save it. A last desperate stand was made at Van Ness Avenue, one of the broadest thoroughfares in the city; a mile-long row of luxurious mansions were ruthlessly dynamited and the fire was halted at that point.

Perhaps the most complete and descriptive account of the double tragedy of earthquake and fire was made by Dr. Ernest W. Fleming, who had been staying at the Palace Hotel, escaped to Los Angeles, and from that point worked with the Chamber of Commerce to bring relief to San Francisco. He gave this all-inclusive account:

I was sleeping in a room on the third floor of the hotel [he said] when the first shock occurred. An earthquake in San Francisco was no new sensation to me. I was there in 1868, a boy of ten, when my first earthquake came. But that was a gentle rocking of a cradle to the one on Wednesday.

I woke to the groaning of timbers, the grinding, creaking and roaring. Plaster and wall decorations fell. The sensation was as though the building were stretching and writhing like a snake. The darkness was intense. Shrieks of women, higher, shriller than that of the creaking timbers, cut the air.

I tumbled from the bed and crawled toward the door. The twisting and writhing appeared to increase. The air was oppressive. I seemed to be saying to myself, "Will it never, never stop?" I wrenched the lock, the door of the room swung back against my shoulder. Just then the building seemed to breathe, stagger and right itself.

I fled from that building as from a falling wall. I could not believe that it could endure such a shock and still stand. The next I remember was standing in the street laughing at the unholy appearance of half a hundred men clad in pajamas and less. The women were in their night robes; they made a better appearance than the men. There was raiment of every hue— and, in many cases, raiment never intended to be seen outside the boudoir.

I looked at a man at my side. He was laughing at me. Then for the first time I became aware that I was in pajamas myself. I turned and fled back to my room. There I dressed, packed my grip, and hastened back to the street.

All the big buildings on Market Street toward the ferry were standing, but I marked four separate fires. The fronts of the small buildings had fallen out into the street and at some places the debris had broken through the sidewalks into cellars.

I noticed two women near me. They were apparently without escort. One said to the other, "What wouldn't I give to be back in Los Angeles again." That awakened a kindred feeling and I proffered my assistance. I put my overcoat on the stone steps of a building and told them to sit there. In less than two minutes those steps appeared to pitch everything forward. The groaning and writhing started afresh.

I was just stunned. I stood there in the street with debris falling all about me. It seemed the natural thing for the tops of buildings to career over and for fronts to fall out. I do not even recall that the women screamed. The street gave a convulsive shudder and the buildings somehow righted themselves again. The two women arose and started to walk. I followed in an aimless sort of way.

The street was filled with moving things again. The rainbow raiment had disappeared, and all were clad in street clothes. Everyone was walking but there was no confusion. We did not even seem to hurry. We walked down Market Street to the St. Francis Hotel. Fires were burning down toward the ferry, but the Fire Department had turned them. We had faith in the Fire Department. Soon I became aware that squads of soldiers were patrolling the streets. It appeared perfectly natural. I do not think I wondered why they were there.

Men and women were all about us. We looked at each other and talked, even tried lamely to joke. But every few minutes a convulsive quiver swept through the city. Everyone seemed to be shivering. I noticed that the eyes of the men and women were rolling restlessly. Their tones were pitched high. It seemed to grate on my nerves. Then I fell to wondering whether I was talking shrilly too.

The soldiers came and told us to move on. By this time the fire was creeping dangerously close. We would have walked to the ferry. We tried it on a score of streets, but the wall of fire was always there. It seemed to always creep across in front of us. And in front of the fire walked the soldiers. Many times I hired express wagons. We would ride a few blocks and get out on the sidewalk. In not a single instance were we charged more than a reasonable price for the ride.

Once we loitered until the soldiers came up. A rough fellow who had been standing by my side tried to dart through the line of soldiers. A young lieutenant caught him by the coat.

"Here!" he called to his men. "Shoot this man!"

I hurried on without looking back. I don't remember that I heard a shot fired. But at the time it seemed so trivial a matter that I did not pay much attention.

All the while we were moving onward with the crowd. Cinders were falling about us. At times our clothing caught fire— just little embers that smoked once and went out. The sting burned our faces, and we used our handkerchiefs for veils. Everybody around us was using some kind of cloth to shield their eyes.

Quite naturally we seemed to come to Golden Gate Park. It seemed as though we had started for there. By this time the darkness was setting. But it was a weird twilight. The glare from the burning city threw a kind of red flame and shadow about us.

The giant holocaust raged for three days and nights before it was finally halted. It was stopped on the west by the dynamiting of buildings on Van Ness Avenue; on the east by the natural barrier of the bay; and on the south by the Southern Pacific railroad yards. When the last embers burned away the damage was assessed. It was the most costly double disaster ever visited upon an American city.

The statistics were numbing: 490 city blocks destroyed, 32 others partially ruined; more than 28,000 buildings crumbled or burned out; property loss estimated at $500,000,000; and the death toll approximately 450 with many injured.

But San Franciscans rolled up their sleeves and went to work to revive the stricken city. Civic committees grappled with such problems as relief, finance, reconstruction and transportation. Cities all across the nation sent aid. Help came from Congress and from wealthy individuals.

Rebuilding started immediately. A new water system provided separate mains for public use and for fighting fires. Reservoirs were built around the city, and a more effective system for pumping salt water from the bay into the city was devised.

Within three years San Francisco was completely rebuilt. The earthquake and fire had proved to be only a temporary step backward in the city's march of progress.

3

The Good Friday Catastrophe
Alaska (1964)

A few years ago I stood at Knik Arm, west of Anchorage, Alaska, and gazed out over 135 acres of tortured earth that had been left by Alaska's great earthquake of 1964. A sign, marking the spot, read as follows:

"And behold the earth did quake and the rocks rent."— St. Matthews account of the first Good Friday Earthquake. This broken ground stands in evidence of the Good Friday Earthquake of March 27, 1964—the strongest ever recorded on the North American continent, registering between 8.4 and 8.6 on the Richter scale. During four minutes of violent shaking that began at 5:36 P.M., approximately 24,000 square miles of the earth's surface was raised or lowered an average of three to eight feet along a 500-mile arc centered upon the quake's epicenter in Prince William Sound, 100 miles to the east. The quake triggered a massive earth slide in this area which, beginning a few hundred yards to the east, destroyed many homes and carried their remains over the collapsing bluff. Loss of life here and in other hard-hit Alaskan communities, both from the quake and ensuing seismic sea waves, totalled 115. Property loss was estimated at about a half billion dollars. Youthful Alaskans, grateful for the generosity and unprecedented assistance extended by the rest of the nation and the whole world, were quick to pick up the pieces, rebuild their shattered communities and get on with the development of America's Last Frontier.

Anchorage—today Alaska's largest and most modern city—had a humble beginning, serving as construction headquarters for the Alaska Railroad in 1914. Situated on a high bluff overlooking Knik Arm, a branch of Cook Inlet, Anchorage lies as far west as the Hawaiian Islands and as far north as Helsinki, Finland. Forming an unforgettable backdrop for the city are the jagged peaks of the Alaska Range on the northeast and the massive Chugach Mountains on the east.

By the fateful year of 1964, Anchorage had firmly established itself as the business center of the State of Alaska. In appearance, it was a combination of urban sophistication and frontier ruggedness. The big-city image was supported by 25 hotels and as many motels, 60 churches, two theaters, a number of high-rise apartment buildings, 26 elementary and high schools with a total enrollment of 16,000 students, two colleges, and an international airport that was the focal point for polar flights to Europe and Asia. All this was superimposed on a more primitive Anchorage, with its crude cabin-like homes and old-fashioned saloons with garish fronts that strongly implied that they were for men only.

Because of its relatively mild climate (averaging eleven degrees above zero in January, its coldest month), the area around Anchorage was one of the most popular winter sports centers in the state. Facilities for ice skating, skiing, curling, ice hockey and dogsled racing attracted thousands, and Anchorage itself served as the outfitting center for big-game hunting on the Kenai Peninsula and in the Rainy Pass region.

Good Friday, March 27, 1964, was a mild day with temperatures in the 20s. Snow covered the city with a thin white blanket. The after-five exodus from the business center was lighter than usual because of the holiday. Most of the people who had attended Tre Ore services had returned to their homes; a few had stayed downtown to shop at stores that had reopened for business at three o'clock. The schools were closed and most of the children were home, although the Fourth Avenue Theater was entertaining a large audience of youngsters at a matinee showing of a Walt Disney film. Many women, expecting the arrival of their husbands from work, were busy preparing the evening meal and looking forward to a calm and peaceful weekend.

This was the scene at 5:36 P.M., when the earthquake struck. It was the most violent quake ever recorded on the North American continent—stronger than San Francisco's upheaval in 1906, and perhaps as strong as the unmeasured New Madrid quake of 1811, although it was not as long in duration. The savage shaking lasted no more than four minutes.

The Great Alaska Earthquake, as it has come to be called, originated some 30 miles below the surface of Prince William Sound, east of Anchorage. From this focal point it traveled with incredible speed, racing across the face of the earth at what has been described as "thousands of miles an hour." It sent huge tidal waves (tsunamis) crashing into coastal towns in Alaska, along the west coast of the contiguous United States, and as far away as the Hawaiian Islands. The ground rose a dozen feet in some places and sank as much in others. Highways were ruptured and railroad tracks twisted into pretzel shapes. Great mountains trembled and high cliffs crumbled in awesome landslides. In Anchorage, Valdez, Seward, Kodiak and other towns, buildings were turned into instant rubble, homes demolished, streets torn up, electric light poles felled.

Anchorage was the hardest hit of the cities. Here the first

shocks struck with special savagery. In the downtown area the quake literally ripped the ground from beneath homes and commercial buildings. In the northwest part of the city a strange horizontal landslide—called a block glide by geologists—rearranged a ten-block area. The earth, moving laterally, actually transplanted homes caught in the center of the glide while shattering those at either end. One six-story apartment building in this area was moved ten feet, sustaining virtually no damage.

To the east, another similar block glide occurred when a 120-foot bluff moved laterally, crushing a fuel storage tank and damaging a hospital. In more level portions of the city great fissures opened in the ground, and one elementary school, standing on a line of earth cracks, was destroyed. Its east wing collapsed in a heap as the south wing dropped 30 feet.

But the most concentrated devastation in Anchorage occurred in two locations—the downtown section along Fourth Avenue and the wealthy Turnagain Heights subdivision in the western part of the city.

In downtown Anchorage the quake worked quickly and with deadly results. Fourth Avenue—the main street of stores, business offices, theaters, cafes and amusement centers—was leveled. In less than a second the quake traveled its length, scissoring the ground from beneath buildings and dropping them into crevices. Some buildings crumbled; others simply settled downward. As one citizen said, "It was like pulling a rug from beneath someone's feet—everything just fell down."

One man, trying to stand as the street rocked beneath him, stared in amazement as the line of buildings toppled like dominoes. A woman watched in similar dismay as snake-like fissures opened in the street, some of them twelve feet deep and fifty feet wide. "The earth rolled for about five minutes," she said. "It slammed parked cars together. People were clinging to each other, to lamp posts, to buildings." In some cases the quake played capricious tricks. The Denali Theater, in the line of Fourth Avenue buildings, dropped ten feet, with only its marquee visible. A florist shop was ripped in half, but Easter flowers in delicate vases were left untouched.

A new six-story apartment building, as yet untenanted, caved in under the severe shock waves. A large department store swayed, managed not to collapse, but was damaged inside and out. A complex of split-level apartments was torn apart and several high-rise buildings badly damaged. In all, a 30-block area of downtown Anchorage was ravaged.

Alice Shoemaker, a secretary, was in her eleventh floor apartment:

> I had come home from work [she said] and was getting ready to go out to eat. I was running a bathtub of water and had set out my clothes. First there was a slight shake and I didn't think much about it since they are fairly common here. Then it got worse. The water slopped out of the bathtub and ran all over the floor. I began looking around. All the kitchen utensils, groceries in the cabinet, books and everything rolled back and forth across the floor with me as I fell down and rolled. When the wall began to give, I thought that was it. I thought, "I'm eleven floors up and can't get out." I started praying, "Oh, God, help me, help me." Finally, when it quit, I opened the door and a woman was lying in the hall holding her baby and screaming. Finally she got up. All the lights were out. I ran to the stairwell. When I opened the door I could see by the dim light coming in through the window a heap of children and their mothers lying on the landing below. They were sobbing and crying. I guess they tried to get out too soon and were pitched down the stairs by the shock.

Joe Marboe, manager of the Fourth Avenue Theater, was working at his desk. Some 700 children were watching the end of the matinee movie. Suddenly the building began to shake and the lights went out. The screen blackened and the lobby was plunged into darkness.

Marboe acted quickly. He switched on standby power and the lights came on again. Then he rushed to the auditorium, directed ushers to stand in the aisles and avert a dangerous rush to the doors. Then he climbed up on the stage.

"Stay in your seats!" he shouted. "Don't move! It's an earthquake and it will be over in a minute."

Later Marboe said, "I believe the children were more scared of me than they were of the earthquake, because we had no panic, and we had no one leaving their seats during the whole time."

Fortunately the theater was not damaged severely and none of the children were lost.

Carol Tucker was shopping on the third floor of Anchorage's newest department store when porcelain figurines began to dance lifelike on the counter. She had experienced quakes before and, like a well-drilled soldier, she crossed the trembling floor to the escalators. Before she reached them the lights went out.

Groping about, she located an escalator and started down. At one point she stumbled and fell, but she managed to escape the building as portions of it began to disintegrate. She narrowly missed being killed as she left the building when huge sections of the facade crashed to the ground, burying a man and a woman.

Mrs. Milo Fritz, wife of an eye specialist with offices in downtown Anchorage, described the quake this way: "I heard a roar at first. I came out of a swaying doorway, swaying myself. Then I was struck by the complete silence, broken only by the tinkle of glass. I saw a 60-foot high building sink slowly fifteen feet into the ground like an elevator stage in a theater."

In Turnagain Heights, the quiet Good Friday afternoon was changed, within seconds, into a chaotic nightmare. Here most of Anchorage's well-to-do citizens lived on a high bluff overlooking Knik Arm that provided them with a spectacular view of Alaskan scenery. Most of the neighborhood's women and children were home. The quake started imperceptibly, with a gentle shaking. But this deceptive rocking movement lasted only seconds. Then an ominous rumble was heard and the ground began to roll in rippling waves.

Those who had experienced Alaskan tremors over the years, sensing that something of major proportions was about to take place, rushed from their homes, with no time to dress against the 20-degree temperatures outside. Some of the children were even barefooted. Those who stayed indoors—either by choice or because the rolling floor prevented them from leaving—were crushed as their houses collapsed.

Fissures formed a crazy pattern in the ground, and the high bluff, on which the houses perched, trembled. Suddenly the bluff began to disintegrate; a section 4,300 feet long collapsed. In this mammoth land displacement 75 houses were destroyed; some were reduced to wreckage that clung to what was left of the bluff while others cascaded 35 feet down the crumbling slope to the sea. Entire streets, automobiles, garages and people were caught up in the landslide.

Great fissures opened on what was left of the bluff. Houses were torn apart by the gaping crevices, roofs caved in, and the earth sank six feet before the quake lost its power. When the shocks finally ceased, Turnagain Heights had become a tumbled ruin. From the breakaway line where the bluff crumbled, winding cracks had traveled inland for more than 2,000 feet, ripping down homes in their path.

Mrs. Lowell Thomas, Jr., daughter-in-law of the noted broadcaster and world traveler, lived through the Turnagain landslide. With her husband in Fairbanks on business, she was alone with her two small children in their bluff-side home. Small earthquakes had been a part of her life, but this sudden low rumbling seemed more ominous than most.

With her children in tow, she raced out the door. Glass shattered, wood creaked, and the house crumbled in a heap behind them.

Now the earth shook so violently that all three of them were thrown into a snowbank. As they cowered there, trees crashed to earth, the ground broke into chunks, and writhing, snake-like cracks opened up all around them. One fissure split the ground between Mrs. Thomas and her daughter, but she was able to grab the child and pull her to safety.

The worst was still to come. All at once the bank on which the house was built collapsed and Mrs. Thomas and her children were carried downward in a huge landslide. Miraculously, they fell to sea level without injury, but here the danger was compounded. As the new face of the cliff above continued to crumble, huge chunks of falling earth and rock threatened to bury them.

At this moment the jolting of the earth stopped; the landslide ceased; the ground beneath them steadied. Mrs. Thomas decided there was only one way out. She and the children would have to climb the new-born cliff to safety. It seemed impossible until a group of men appeared at the top of the cliff and, with ropes, managed to pull them to safety.

Mrs. Rubia Tikka and her husband, a high school chemistry teacher, were driving along the Seward Highway about five miles from Anchorage. With them were their four oldest children and a niece. They had been skiing at a resort 35 miles from Anchorage and were hurrying home to pick up their two youngest children who had spent the day with a neighbor in the Turnagain section.

All at once the car lurched. "We thought we had a flat tire," Mrs. Tikka said later. "Then we knew it had to be an earthquake. Seward Highway was pitching and heaving back and forth and great cracks opened across it."

The drive was a frightening adventure. Time after time Mr. Tikka had to order everyone out on the road as he gingerly maneuvered his car around jagged fissures and piles of debris. When they finally reached Anchorage, they discovered, to their horror, that the house where their children had been staying had been leveled. Frantically they searched the wrecked neighborhood, until they found their youngsters unharmed in a house that had not been damaged.

"We were told later that the first shock had opened a fissure across the front of our neighbor's house," Mrs. Tikka said. "My neighbor just grabbed the children and threw them across the fissure into a snowbank. Then she jumped across herself."

That night the Tikkas slept with thirty other people on the floor of the still-standing house. The next day they found their own home extensively damaged.

"Before the quake," Mrs. Tikka said, "our house was two-and-a-half blocks from a big bluff called Turnagain-by-the-Sea. Afterward, it was right on the edge of the bluff. The land in between had just dropped away."

Milton Norton, a young geologist, was at home with his family in the Turnagain Heights subdivision. "We were looking out the back when we noticed the first tremor moving in an east-west direction," he said. "We paid little notice at first because earth tremors are by no means rare here. Then suddenly it grew in violence and everything began to shake horribly. We heard trees snapping and houses crunching and smashing. My six-year-old son, Mike, was in the back yard playing with his Eskimo dog. I tried to get out of the house to reach him but couldn't make much progress on the rocking floor. I saw a fissure race toward him—only a foot away. I yelled and he moved away from it."

One prosperous Turnagain Heights resident whose home and possessions were lost refused to give her name to a reporter who questioned her after the quake, but her words were prophetic.

"Unless you can use the names of all the people who suffered here," she said, "please don't use mine. I'm no better and probably not much worse than any of the others who lost everything. I'm going to start all over. So will they."

In a large perimeter around Anchorage the shuddering earth put on an awesome show of force. In many mercifully unpopulated areas the land was dramatically changed. Great snow avalanches thundered down mountain sides, an estimated year's quota of avalanches occurring within a few minutes. More than 50 rock slides, covering areas as wide as a mile, plunged down on top of age-old glaciers. The most spectacular of these was at Sherman Glacier, 170 miles southeast of Anchorage and only seven miles from the Cordova airport. In one of history's greatest upheavals 13 million cubic yards of rock from two mountains crashed down on top of the glacier. The slide covered three square miles of the glacier's surface with a layer of mixed rock, earth and ice, three to ten feet deep.

Several small coastal towns suffered two-pronged attacks—first, the violent shaking of the quake, and second, an upheaval from the sea. Valdez, a port city of about 1,000 people, squats on an inlet some 30 miles from Prince William Sound. Hemmed in by snow-capped mountains, it is a scenic city that proudly calls itself the "Switzerland of America." When the first jolts rose up from the depths of Prince William Sound, the town shook as if in the grip of some cosmic hand. The usual destruction took place—houses and stores caved in, the water and sewage systems were disrupted, small boats in the harbor flipped over, cracks rippled across the streets.

The second act of Valdez's catastrophe came in the form of a giant tidal wave, or tsunami, churned up by the underwater quake. It came roaring up the inlet toward the town, a towering, unstoppable, wall of water. Residents tried to flee to higher ground, but they had little chance. On the pier at the time were some twenty stevedores and onlookers, including a man and his two children who were watching the workmen. The tsunami crashed over them; both people and pier vanished. It swept into Valdez, carrying with it houses, stores, and people. A few souls managed to reach safety, but many others were swamped by the wave and, when the tsunami eventually spent its fury and the backwash occurred, wreckage and human bodies were carried into the sea. The double attack left 32 people dead and the town's fishing industry annihilated.

Kodiak was even harder hit; it was pounded by at least a dozen waves, three of them monstrous. Located on the northeast tip of Kodiak Island, some 250 miles southwest of Anchorage, Kodiak was particularly vulnerable because it was built on flat land only twenty feet above sea level. Its 4,200 residents, including United States Navy personnel from the Kodiak Naval Station a few miles away, depended on the sea for their livelihood. The four major and dozen small seafood processing plants were the town's principal industry.

Curiously enough, the earthquake itself caused only minor damage in Kodiak. A few homes collapsed, some were moved off their foundations, a high school was damaged, telephone and power service was disrupted, but there was no loss of life. The tidal waves that followed, however, created havoc.

Karl Armstrong, editor of the *Kodiak Mirror,* was in a drugstore when the quake jarred the city. When the tremors stopped he returned to his office and attempted to phone an account of the quake to Anchorage. Unable to get through, he became perturbed, not realizing that the tremors in Kodiak were part of a much larger quake, and drove to the Naval Station seeking a line that would work.

Peter M. Deveau, who served as mayor of Kodiak and managed a king-crab cannery, was at dockside when he felt a curious thump. Thinking a misguided crab-boat had slammed into the dock, he went outside to investigate just as a heavier shock occurred that almost swept him off his feet. Deveau went to the nearest phone and called home, telling his wife that she should get food and blankets and head for Pillar Mountain. "I figured anything this violent might start a tidal wave," he explained afterward.

Unlike the events at Valdez, there was no immediate tidal wave from the sea. The first tsunami did not hit the city until an hour after the quake. During that hour every effort was made to warn the populace that tsunamis were expected. Fire trucks sounded their sirens, a shore patrol truck raced through the city urging residents to flee to higher ground, and the Naval Station put out warnings on radio and television. Undoubtedly, lives were saved by these timely warnings, for many people headed for Pillar Mountain. Others, however, stayed in the city, underestimating the danger and wanting to "see the sights" when the waves came in.

The first wave itself served as a mild warning. It was not a gigantic wall of water such as the one that had submerged Valdez. It came in silently, like a rising tide, traveling with speed but having no crest, more like a gentle flood than a ravaging tsunami. It delicately transported the fishing boats that were near shore onto dry land, did other minor damage, and then flowed back into the sea. The floodtide had been just big enough to convince thinking people to move to Pillar Mountain, and just small enough to reassure the heedless that the town was in little danger.

A few minutes later the sea returned, this time seemingly with calculated vengeance. A monstrous wall of water with a crest 30 feet high roared up the channel. Crab boats weighing 50 to 100 tons were lifted high and hurled violently ashore, coming to rest several blocks inland. Cannery buildings tumbled under the assault and within minutes most of the king-crab fishing center was wiped off the map. Karl Armstrong, unsuccessful in his search for a telephone to Anchorage, was back in town by this time and witnessed the second tsunami. "You could hear it coming," he said. "Then it poured over the breakwater and into the boat harbor. The boat harbor all of a sudden was higher than the town. You could see all the boats riding high up in the air. Then they moved—right into town."

Bill Cuthbert, skipper of a king-crab boat called the *Selief*, went for a wild ride. His boat, bouncing like a cork as the great wave struck, finally came to rest three blocks from dockside. As the tsunami receded, a marine operator tried to contact stranded boats by radio. Her call got through to Captain Cuthbert and she asked his location. "By dead reckoning," he said calmly, "I'm in the schoolhouse yard."

The third tsunami waited for 55 minutes before making its appearance. It was higher than the second but rolled in with much less force—enough, though, to beach remaining crab boats and do further damage to canneries, office buildings and homes. The waves continued to move in, with less and less violence each time, until three A.M. the next morning.

Despite the repeated pounding of the tidal waves, casualties in Kodiak were fantastically light. Only eight people died in the city and another dozen in scattered areas of Kodiak Island. But physical damage to property was tremendous. Forty per cent of Kodiak's business district was destroyed and 30 per cent of its fishing industry ruined. The boat harbor was gone, three-fourths of the city's food stocks lost. 158 homes washed away, and the downtown area of the city was a tangled heap of boats, wrecked buildings, automobiles, and general debris carried ashore by the tsunamis.

It is something of a miracle that fire played virtually no part during the Alaskan quakes. Of all the towns ravaged by the earthquake, only Seward suffered from a quake-spawned blaze. Located at the tip of Resurrection Bay on the Gulf of Alaska, Seward had a population of 2,000 people in 1964 and was the southern terminus of The Alaska Railroad and the transfer point for cargo coming in by ship. On its expansive docks, oil and other products were transferred to railroad cars and shuttled as far as 500 miles inland. Along the waterfront, close to the railroad tracks, were oil tanks owned by Texaco and Standard Oil—an arrangement that was to prove disastrous to the bustling little town on the bay.

When the first shock of the late-afternoon earthquake rocked Seward, people ran into the open streets. The town seemed to be dancing crazily around them. Some homes caved in, brick buildings fell, and more sturdy structures swayed like thin-stemmed plants. The ground rolled in sickening waves and crevices opened in the street. But, most threatening of all, one of the Standard Oil tanks exploded, spraying fire to other tanks and eventually igniting the entire waterfront.

To add to the fiery horror, a 40-foot-high tsunami smashed into Seward twenty minutes after the shaking subsided. People fled in all directions to escape the deluge, even though some hoped that the great seismic wave might be what was needed to put out the fire raging on the waterfront. But instead of extinguishing the blaze, the tsunami spread it. Water swept into the dock area, picked up flaming debris and carried it inland. The wave's fiery top scattered the flames all over town, setting fire to homes and commercial buildings. As it receded it dragged railroad cars, houses and other wreckage out to sea.

Gene Kirkpatrick, a railroad man, described the scene. "When the fire was really roaring," he related, "the wave came up Resurrection Bay and spread it everywhere. It was an eerie thing to see—a huge tide of fire washing ashore, setting a high-water mark in flame, and then sucking back."

Hundreds of people escaped the initial shock and the following wave by good luck or quick thinking. Two men in the harbor boat-shop heard the groan of timbers as the quake hit and dashed outside just before the building collapsed. Another man escaped from the dock's coffee shop as it began to settle down toward the water. A crane operator, perched 50 feet above The Alaska Railroad dock on a gantry crane, suddenly became aware that his perch was wobbling from side to side. Looking down, he noticed that the crane's opposite wheels were alternately on and off the tracks. Then he saw that the entire dock was beginning to crumble. He quickly descended and managed to flee from the dock area before it plunged into the bay.

Similar escapes marked the arrival of the 40-foot tsunami. Entire families got into their automobiles and outraced the terrifying wave pursuing them. Some fled the wall of water on foot. Still others, unable to reach higher ground, climbed trees and clung perilously in the swaying branches until the tsunami flowed back to the sea. A crewman of the tanker *Alaska Standard* was the beneficiary of a miracle. The giant wave hit him as he stood on one of the docks and knocked him unconscious. When he came to he found that the surge of water had lifted him above the tanker and deposited him on a catwalk eight feet above the deck—unhurt.

Waves continued to pound Seward until almost midnight, and earth shocks jolted the area well into the morning hours. Several more oil tanks blew up; the resulting fire raged for three days before it finally burned itself out. When it was all over the grim job of assessing the damage was undertaken. The triple blows of earthquake, fire and water had killed twelve people—a remarkably low death toll. But the city had been virtually wiped out. Five docks had completely disappeared, including The Alaska Railroad wharfage. Warehouses and a halibut cannery were destroyed. Thirty fishing boats and a like number of pleasure craft had sunk or were broken up. Fire had gutted three homes; the quake and seismic waves had demolished 83 others. Public buildings were badly damaged by fire and water, some beyond repair. Power lines were downed, and the city was unable to communicate with other parts of the state.

The size and violence of the Great Alaska Earthquake was measured by seismographs throughout much of the world. In Pasadena, California, 2,500 miles away, and at the Colorado School of Mines in Golden, Colorado, the forces of nature were too much for the measuring equipment. In both cases, tracings at the height of the quake ran off the scale. A seismograph at Spring Hill College in Mobile, Alabama, registered 8.6 on the Richter Scale, and even in such remote countries as Scotland, England, Finland, and Sweden, seismographs were jolted for hours.

The tsunamis created by the underwater upheaval traveled far and wide. A huge wave hit Port Alberni on Vancouver Island, and poured into the Canadian pulp and logging center there. It also caused heavy water damage to the city's best hotel, flooding the lobby, dining room and kitchen. Santa Catalina Island, twenty miles off the coast of Los Angeles, was hit by a ten-foot-high wave. More than 1,000 people were evacuated from Eureka, California, before a wave swept over the town. In Depoe Bay, Oregon, waves rolled over a family of four on a beach and carried them out to sea. Even Hawaii felt the force of the quake as a series of tidal waves lashed the islands.

Crescent City, California—1,400 miles from the Alaska Peninsula—was particularly hard-hit. Five hours after the quake a seismic wave engulfed a 56-block area of the city, killing 11 people and injuring 59. It still had enough force after its long trip south to knock buildings off their foundations, destroy power facilities, ruin numerous businesses, and indulge in one of nature's typically capricious acts.

Mrs. Mabel Martin of Crescent City was asleep when the water rushed into her small house near the beach. Her bed floated toward the roof and finally lodged under the eaves, the arched rooftop providing just enough air for her to continue breathing. Pressure from the surging waters finally collapsed the walls of the house and the roof floated free. Mrs.

Martin, her bed jammed underneath the eaves, floated with it. The wave carried the roof for two-and-one-half blocks before the water receded. Mrs. Martin, still trapped, cried for help. She was not discovered until seven hours after the wave hit—damp but unhurt.

Actually, a happy combination of circumstances kept the death toll in the Alaskan earthquake relatively light, despite the severity of the quake and the extensive physical damage. There were several reasons for this: the population was sparse; the quake struck on a holiday afternoon when schools were empty and most offices closed; the tide had been abnormally low and, although tsunamis ravaged many places, a high tide would have added to the problem; electrical facilities in Anchorage and other areas were the first to be knocked out, reducing the hazard of fire; and mild weather helped to ward off pneumonia and other diseases that might have occurred had unhoused people been exposed to low temperatures.

Within a few months of Alaska's tragedy, the hardy citizens of the 49th state had cleaned up the rubble and were rapidly rebuilding. Badly damaged Anchorage eventually became a larger and more flourishing city than ever, and the peripheral towns also fought back. Tough, durable, and with a sense of humor, the Alaskans even joked about the disaster as they worked. A bar in the city of Anchorage concocted two new drinks named "All Shook Up" and "The Fourth Avenue Splits." One wag published a song book with phony titles, such as "Standing on the Corner Watching All the Streets Divide." And it became customary for people to kid each other about living on the wrong side of the cracks.

But the Great Alaskan Earthquake of 1964 was by no stretch of the imagination a joke. Alaskans will be quite content not to have another one.

Hurricane!

In a general sense, the word hurricane can be used to describe any violent windstorm. More specifically, the term is applied to the tropical revolving storm common to the Caribbean. Other names are used in other regions: in the Bay of Bengal and the Arabian Sea these heavy blows are called cyclones; in the China seas, typhoons; and in Australia, willy-willies.

To qualify as a true hurricane, the rampaging winds must exceed 75 miles an hour (12 on the Beaufort scale). Often they reach speeds as high as 150 miles an hour. The area of high velocity winds seldom is more than 500 miles across, and the winds rotate around a calm center known as the eye of the hurricane. In the northern hemisphere the winds revolve around this center counter-clockwise and in the southern hemisphere clockwise—a condition known as the Coriolis effect. This circulation of air often reaches elevations as high as 10,000 feet and has been known to extend into the stratosphere.

The eye of the hurricane is a meteorological phenomenon not found in any other type of storm. As the hurricane moves over a given point, the region is whipped by wild winds capable of great destruction. Then, as the eye of the hurricane approaches, the winds die down dramatically, often diminishing to fifteen miles an hour or less. The slashing rains cease and quite often the sun shines through. But the eye represents only a momentary lull; the other side of the hurricane's circumference resumes its destruction. This time, however, direction of the winds is reversed.

Most Caribbean hurricanes develop from June to October, when the surface of the sea is warmest and air humidity highest—a combination that spawns tropical storms. Normally there are about eight tropical blows a year, five of which reach hurricane proportions, with September and October the peak months for such activity. Raging out of the Caribbean, these storms can do one of three things: blow themselves out over the Atlantic Ocean; turn inland toward the Florida coast; or veer westward into the Gulf of Mexico. A few even reach the New England states before dying out.

All hurricanes are accompanied by cumulus and cumulo nimbus clouds that bring from three to six inches of torrential rain. These downpours can cause severe flooding in inland areas, and the winds may produce disastrous waves that inundate coastal regions.

Naming hurricanes after females began in the 1940s. Although some women have complained that this is a libel on their sex, the U. S. Weather Bureau insists that no slight is intended. The practice stems from World War II, when typhoons in the Pacific were given names in order to insure that messages about them were transmitted accurately. Identifying storms by longitude and latitude was awkward, and numbering them was confusing. And lonely soldiers being lonely soldiers, they gave the storms women's names.

The Weather Bureau did not begin the practice until September 1950, when three hurricanes roamed the Caribbean at the same time. As a result, the labeling of storms came back into prominence and the habit of giving them female names was eventually followed.

4

The Storm That Killed 8,000

Galveston, Texas (1900)

Almost every autumn, hurricanes spawned in the south Atlantic roar up through the Caribbean and aim their Sunday punches at such exposed areas of the United States as the Florida peninsula and the coastal regions of the Gulf of Mexico. Inevitably these monster storms cause widespread property damage and death: 327 killed in Florida and Alabama in 1926; 600 dead when a hurricane swept north clear to the New England states in 1938; 400 killed along the eastern seaboard by Hurricane *Diane* in 1955; 430 by *Audrey* in 1957; 258 by *Camille* in 1969.

But in terms of death and destruction these terrible blows were dwarf-storms compared to the violent tempest of wind and water that struck unprotected Galveston, Texas, on September 8, 1900. In that frightening storm—the most disastrous in American history—winds blowing up to 130 miles an hour swept angry Gulf waters over the entire city of Galveston and its terrified population of 38,000. Two-thirds of the 5,400 homes in the city were completely destroyed by monstrous twenty-foot waves, and half of the business section was leveled. In Galveston alone 6,000 people were killed, and along the nearby Texas coast an additional 2,000 met watery deaths.

Most of Galveston's population was apathetic about the storm rolling in from the Gulf. Aside from battening-down a few hatches and buttoning up a few shutters, people did little to protect themselves from the coming onslaught. They considered the Weather Bureau warnings to be of concern only to fishermen; after all, the citizens of Galveston had weathered Gulf storms before, and this would be just another overflow—their term for a slightly-higher-than-usual tide.

Isaac M. Cline, chief of the Galveston Weather Bureau, was one of the few who accurately judged the storm's potential. It was 4 P.M. on September 4, 1900, when he first learned of a threatening hurricane moving north over Cuba. It was September 7 when he heard that the storm had slithered past the southern tip of Florida and pointed its angry nose at Galveston. Since these were radio-less days, Cline warned the city's inhabitants by telephone and signal flags that rough weather was in prospect.

On Saturday morning, September 8, ominous gray clouds moved over the city and heavy rains began to fall. Alarmed, Cline set out in a horsedrawn wagon and rode up and down the beaches warning people to seek higher ground. Then he returned to the Weather Bureau offices, where he kept one eye on the falling barometer and the other on the slate-gray clouds boiling over the city. All this time he was torn between his obligation to stay at his post and his desire to be with his wife and three children, who awaited the brunt of the storm at home.

No such worries concerned Dr. S. O. Young, who had a home near Galveston Beach. That Saturday morning he rose early to watch the already large waves pound the beach. He had phoned his wife, who was staying in San Antonio, and told her not to return to Galveston because of the developing storm, but he was sure that his staunch home would withstand the worst the hurricane could offer. He spent an hour that morning walking along the beach, then retired to his front porch to view nature's spectacle with a detached and scientific eye. This, he thought, would be an interesting show.

Daisy Thorne, a young school teacher, prepared an early morning breakfast for herself and her mother in her third-floor apartment. She was only slightly apprehensive about the storm. Her apartment was three blocks from the Gulf, and from her elevated porch she calmly took photographs of the great waves sweeping the beach. She had heard the Weather Bureau warnings and conceded that the waves were somewhat larger than usual—but, surely, a 64-family apartment building like the Lucas Terrace was a safe refuge from the most violent winds and heaviest rains.

In her comfortable home at Hunt Street and F Avenue, Sarah Humes noted that the storm was growing in violence and thought first of her valuables. She owned a considerable amount of jewelry, which she prized highly, and she quickly gathered all of her precious gems together. She was determined that, whatever might happen before this day was finished, her jewels would be secure.

John Matti, a grocer, went to his store that morning aware that a storm was brewing but still expecting a brisk Saturday business. But as the wind velocity increased he found that customers were scarce and he considered closing up and going home. He stalled for awhile, hoping that business would improve, but by noontime he found the water two feet deep in the streets and people wading anxiously about trying to reach higher ground.

At Saint Mary's Orphanage, Mother Superior Camillus,

the nuns and the orphans prayed in the chapel as the storm swept the city. Before noon the water seeped through the chapel door and drove them to an upstairs room. Mother Superior Camillus recognized that the day's "overflow" was greater than any she had ever seen, but she was sure that the storm would abate shortly and that the sturdy orphanage would withstand the winds.

Elsewhere in the city, people went about their usual tasks. Most of the men left for work and wives occupied themselves with household tasks. Some mothers, hearing about the giant swells crashing on the beach, actually took their children to the water's edge to see the view.

Galveston, in 1900, was a pleasant semitropical city of white buildings, oleander-lined streets, softly swaying palm trees, and contented citizens. One of the most beautiful beaches in the world attracted vacationers from many miles around. The Beach Hotel provided lavish accommodations for people with large bankrolls, and Murdock's Restaurant overlooking the surf was *the* place to dine. Bettison's Pier was a fishing establishment of considerable note, and a place called the Pagoda was a popular bathing pavilion. Pat O'Keefe's famous beach resort and Galveston's largest hotel, The Tremont, attracted throngs all summer. Besides being a resort town of major importance, Galveston was a fast-growing port from which millions of dollars worth of cotton and grain were exported annually.

Low and sandy Galveston Island, on which the city of Galveston is situated, is 28 miles long and from two to three miles wide, stretching along the Texas coast from northeast to southwest. In 1900, it was separated from the mainland by Galveston Bay, a ribbon of water two miles wide spanned by three bridges. At no point on this huge sandbar is the land higher that 8.7 feet above high tide. Broadway marks the center of Galveston, running proudly along the highest ridge, from which the land gently slopes to the Gulf on one side and Galveston Bay on the other.

The fateful morning of September 8 found the hurricane poised 50 miles from Galveston. On its long trip from the Windward Islands, past Jamaica and Cuba and into the Gulf of Mexico, the West Indies-spawned storm had steadily increased in power. By the time it reached Galveston it was at its peak of intensity.

The hurricane alone would have been a catastrophe for Galveston, but a freak of nature was impending that would deepen the disaster. While the hurricane punched at the eastern side of the island, a northwest gale began to lash the opposite side, blowing the waters of Galveston Bay across the hapless city. Thus Galveston Island became a pawn in a battle of the elements. It was recognized early that if the "norther" held against the fury of the hurricane, Galveston would survive with few problems. If the hurricane got the upper hand, however, the city was in dire trouble.

During the first half of the tragic Saturday, the "norther" did manage to hold against the might of the West Indies blow. But shortly after noon it began to succumb to the hurricane's greater strength. Like a spinning top caught in a side wind, the "norther" slowly swung clockwise and added its fury to that of the hurricane.

By three o'clock the savage winds were pounding the stricken city with battering-ram force. At 3:40 P.M. Cline sent out the last report from the Weather Bureau: barometric pressure 29:22, wind blowing at a rate of 42 miles an hour. A few minutes later all communication between Galveston and the outside world was abruptly cut off.

At 4 o'clock the hurricane shifted slightly and began hitting Galveston directly from the east with winds of 60 miles an hour. By 5:15 wind velocity had reached 84 miles an hour, at which time the wind gauge on the roof of the Weather

Bureau blew away. Observers estimated that the winds then increased to 120 miles an hour and, in some sectors, hit 130 for brief moments before the storm ebbed.

Storms have wrecked other cities besides Galveston, but it is doubtful that any storm ever did the job more systematically. As if guided by a vengeful intelligence, it began to demolish the city block by block. First the hurricane drove huge twenty-foot waves across the beaches and against the line of homes stretched along the Gulf. Unable to withstand the force of the wind and waves, buildings in the first block along the beach shuddered, sagged, and collapsed. People in this first block of houses were trapped. If they fled, they would be swept away by the waves. If they stayed, they would be crushed to death. There appeared to be no way out—and most of them found no way out.

Having broken large homes like match-sticks and carried smaller structures off in the air, the hurricane then ruthlessly demonstrated its efficiency. The storm proceeded to use the wreckage from the demolished first block, pushing it forward and slamming it against the second row of houses. When the second row collapsed, the great mass of wreckage was hurled against the third block, and then the accumulated debris was driven furiously against the fourth block. Thus, the homes of thousands of people were destroyed systematically and almost all those who remained in this exposed area lost their lives.

By the time this destruction had progressed several blocks, the mass of debris was a terrible and fantastic jumble of houses, bathtubs, sewing machines, stoves, furniture, roof slates and human bodies.

At last the destruction reached Q Street, which was on slightly higher ground. The water, now fourteen feet deep, and the moving mountain of wreckage were still being pushed sluggishly along by the relentless waves. On Q Street there was a line of large mansions, solidly built and offering more resistance than the storm had as yet encountered. As though infuriated at this obstacle, the giant storm hurled the debris with sledge-hammer force against the large homes. But they failed to yield.

Again and again the waves battered the mansions with their warhead of wreckage. The debris piled higher and higher, reaching the eaves of the homes—and at this point nature out-foxed herself. The towering accumulation of wreckage now actually formed a protective wall against the great waves from the Gulf. Water seeped through to flood the portion of the city between Q Street and the bay, but the debris piled against the stalwart mansions spared that part of the city from the brunt of the storm.

Dazed by the hurricane's assault, the people of Galveston fought, struggled, and died without quite understanding how this could happen to them. By mid-afternoon, streets were flooded and men struggled waist-deep trying to get their families and belongings to higher ground. Most of them did not know that there was no ground in Galveston high enough to be completely safe, nor did they realize that all three bridges connecting the city with the mainland were already down.

Many pushed their way into the lobby of the big Tremont Hotel, but even here they were not secure. Late in the afternoon the walls of the hotel shook and water gushed through the front door, spreading menacingly across the lobby. Frantically the crowd moved upstairs, filling the mezzanine, praying and crying as they watched the water fill the ornate lobby below to a depth of three feet. It would not have encouraged them to know that at that moment water covered virtually every inch of Galveston Island.

As in all natural catastrophes, there were acts of both heroism and cowardice. Many people risked their lives to rescue strangers from the relentless flood of water. Others fought like animals for places on floating wreckage, kicking and shoving in feverish attempts to save themselves. In the black hours before midnight, death and destruction reached its peak—large buildings toppled, churches and public buildings vanished, and thousands of people died unseen in the darkness.

Cline of the Weather Bureau stuck to his post until late in the day; then, plagued by doubts about his family's safety, he slogged to his home through waist-deep water against howling winds. To his surprise he found the house still standing and his wife, three daughters and a brother still safe. Before long he had provided shelter for about fifty dazed refugees who stumbled into his home. Later Cline wrote a Weather Bureau report that described the situation.

"The water rose at a steady rate," it reads, "from 3 P.M. until about 7:30 P.M. when there was a sudden rise of about four feet in as many seconds. I was standing at my front door, which was partly open, watching the water which was flowing with great rapidity from east to west. The water at this time was about eight inches deep in my residence and the sudden rise to four feet brought it above my waist before I could change my position."

Not long after, Cline's home collapsed. Thirty-two persons were killed, including Cline's wife. Struggling desperately in the swirling waters, Cline and his brother managed to get themselves and Cline's three children atop some floating wreckage. For two perilous hours they clung to the debris until it at last was washed against a still-standing building, where they safely weathered the rest of the storm.

Daisy Thorne, the school teacher who lived in the 64-family apartment three blocks from the beach, was joined in her room by 22 other tenants. The huge Lucas Terrace had begun to break up under the impact of wind and waves. Room by room the apartment house disintegrated, and each time part of the building broke away Daisy Thorne thought, "This time it will be us."

Eventually only the third-floor room belonging to Miss Thorne remained intact, supported by a flimsy segment of wall. It trembled and wobbled in the storm, but astonishingly the room outlasted the blow and all of the occupants survived. Engineers who studied the remains of the building after the disaster could not explain how this room had managed to remain in one piece.

Dr. Young, who had decided to view nature's rampage from his front porch, found the performance more than he had expected. His frame home was built on brick pillars four feet high, and he had been confident that the structure would not only hold against the wind but would keep the water out. But by four o'clock the ground floor of his house was swamped in two feet of sea water and Dr. Young had been forced to retreat to the second floor, from which, with some trepidation, he watched the rapidly rising flood.

By this time Galveston's electric and gas plants had been put out of commission, so Dr. Young explored the damage to his house by candlelight. He was amazed to find that the water had risen almost to the second story of his home, and that he was now hopelessly marooned.

At the window he watched in horror as several neighboring houses simply disappeared from view in the raging storm. Before long there was only one residence still standing beside his own—that of a neighbor named Youens. As he watched in fascination, the Youens home, hit by a monstrous wave, spun completely around and drifted off.

Soon Dr. Young's house also began to yield to the severe hammering. On one gigantic wave it rose several feet above the ground. Afraid that the building would disintegrate, Dr. Young threw himself from the house into the rushing waters. Grabbing a piece of wreckage, he clung to it while the current drove him at breakneck speed for fifteen blocks. At last he came to an abrupt halt against a mountain of debris, struggled to a home that was still upright and was pulled inside. He was one of the few people living along the beach who survived.

The home of jewelry lover Sarah Humes also began to break up under the pounding waves and whistling winds. Frantic with fear, she ran from room to room, clutching her gems. Suddenly, with a grinding noise, the house caved in. She was found dead the next morning by rescue workers—her hand tightly closed around the jewels.

John Matti, the grocer, decided not to go home at noon and stayed to help the many people wading waist-deep trying to find refuge. He hitched up his horse and wagon and began to rescue his neighbors, taking wagon-load after wagon-load to a nearby firehouse. Several times the wagon of refugees was carried blocks out of the way by the driving waters, but Matti always managed to get back to the firehouse. His heroism, however, came to a tragic end. Just as he was pulling into the firehouse with his last load of refugees, the building crumbled. Most of those he had rescued were killed. So was Matti.

Mother Superior Camillus realized by evening that the Saint Mary's Orphanage building would soon buckle under the force of the hurricane. She called the Sisters together and gave them each a length of rope. Each Sister took eight infants and tied them around her own body. But before they could get away the roof of the orphanage caved in. Most were killed instantly; some fought their way into the swirling current. Only three boys were saved—the Sisters were found later with the dead infants still tied to them.

A 70-year-old-man whose wife and daughter had been lost in the storm, was cast adrift with his dog, a Newfoundland named Hero. True to his name, the swimming dog pulled his frightened master ten blocks through angry waters until they found temporary shelter in a wrecked building. Relief workers discovered them after the storm subsided, but the old man was dead. Hero sat by his side, reluctant to let them remove the body of his master.

At Galveston's Union Depot a crowd of travelers waited in vain to board a train to Houston. Here they were trapped as Galveston's bridges to the mainland were washed away, and when the hurricane increased in intensity they deserted the ground floor and moved into a room on the second level. All of them expected to die because the depot seemed on the verge of collapse innumerable times during a frightening 13-hour stay.

At the height of the vicious storm a few men started to sing a hymn, and soon everyone joined in the refrain. While they sang the wind tore the roof off the depot and blew it away like a scrap of paper, but the rest of the station remained intact and all of the would-be travelers were eventually saved.

A particularly agonizing fate befell Thomas Klee, a young father alone in his home with two infant children. As his frame home on the bayside of the island began to buckle under the savage winds, Klee tucked one child under each arm and waded into the rising waters around his house. Almost at once the current swept him into the bay. But Klee hung onto the two children—a boy, four, and a girl, two— and managed to stay afloat. Noticing a tall tree being swept along by the tide, he swam toward it. His overburdened arms were aching and he had to have a place to station at least one of the children for a few minutes to give himself some relief. The branches of the tree looked like a temporary haven, and he painfully raised his small daughter to a seemingly secure spot. But before he could complete his task a sudden wave tore the child from his grasp and swept her to her death.

Shocked and numbed by the experience, Klee nevertheless managed to hold onto the boy. For the next hour they were carried along by the rapidly flowing water and eventually landed on the mainland of Texas. Klee stumbled ashore.

When he had reached a point of safety, he raised his son high in a gesture of victory. The boy was dead.

The experience of Pat Joyce was typical. There was three feet of water around his home, three blocks from the gulf. He recalled:

> It began to get worse and worse, [Joyce related] with the water getting higher and the wind stronger. Finally the house was taken off its foundation and was entirely demolished. There were nine families in the house, which was a large two-story frame, and of the fifty people residing there my brother and I were the only ones who could get away. We managed to find a raft of driftwood and got on it, drifting with the tide. We had not drifted far before we were stopped by some wreckage, and my brother fell off the raft and was drowned.
>
> I was carried on and on with the tide, sometimes on the raft and again was thrown from it by the waves, but managed to cling to my raft until I was saved. I drifted and swam all night, not knowing where I was going or in what direction. About three o'clock in the morning I began to feel hard ground and I knew I was near land. I got ashore and stumbled to a house nearby. I was in the water about seven hours.

The turning point of the hurricane came at Q Street, where the wreckage had piled high against the immovable mansions. At last the storm had to admit defeat, but by the time the mansions of Q Street held, 5,000 Galvestonians had already died. Another thousand would die before the storm finally spent itself.

At 1:45 on Sunday morning the waves began to subside, and within a half hour the level of water in the city had dropped an average of two feet. Shaken and bewildered, those who still lived crawled from the wreckage to find their city in chaotic ruin.

The streets were no longer streets at all, but debris-strewn lanes that blocked passage. A frightful total of 6,000 human corpses, plus many dead horses and cattle, littered the city.

Many of the victims had been decapitated by roof slates that had sailed through the air like winged knives. Other flying debris had mutilated hundreds beyond recognition. On flooded Tremont Avenue one could cross the street only by stepping on the bodies of the dead. Shocked and confused citizens searched for loved ones. One woman carried her lifeless child in her arms as she wandered aimlessly through the wreckage.

The beach was a misshapen, ravaged thing, strange to the eyes of Galvestonians who had considered it the beauty spot of the city. Great sections had been uprooted by the storm, forming yawning chasms. In the lower districts, along the beach, every home was gone. From the gulf to Avenue P (16 blocks) no house remained in its original position—all had either been moved by the wind and tide or totally destroyed. Twenty per cent of the population had perished in a 13-hour period, and property damage stood at $20,000,000. Even the dead were not spared—coffins were unearthed by the hurricane and their grisly contents scattered about. A green slime, inches deep, covered most of the battered city.

The luxurious Beach Hotel was demolished. The Pagoda bathing pavilion was wrecked. The Home of the Friendless was washed away, with 500 inmates drowned. The Seely Hospital was a crumbled heap in which 100 patients were buried. St. Mary's Orphanage was gone, and St. Mary's Infirmary scuttled. Bettison's fishing pier was a mass of wreckage. Most of the school buildings and churches sheltering refugees were down, and eight steamships in the harbor had been driven onto land and smashed by the waves.

In the deadly stillness following the storm it was noticed that birds and winged insects had disappeared—driven inland by the wind. But soon, attracted by the stench of 6,000 bodies decaying in a semitropical sun that miraculously lighted the scene, billions of flies swooped down—and the fear of plague swept the stricken city.

Recognizing the further disaster that pestilence could bring, martial law was imposed and the grim task of removing the bodies began. There was no time for decent burial. Soldiers with rifles forced burial crews, wearing masks and camphor balls under their noses, to load corpses on drays for transport to tugs and barges in the Gulf. Hysterical crowds at the waterfront had to be stopped from searching for relatives and friends among the stacked bodies.

But even mass burial at sea didn't work flawlessly. Many improperly weighted bodies were washed to shore. Finally it was decided to burn all bodies. Great funeral pyres—one of which contained more than one thousand corpses—appeared all over the city, raising a shroud of dank smoke above the ruins.

As in all disasters, some sought to profit. Scavengers stole jewelry from bodies and looted buildings, and the orders went out to shoot them on sight. Seventy men caught robbing the dead were executed. Most of them had their pockets stuffed with fingers cut from bodies that had swollen too much to permit easy removal of rings. Some pockets were filled with ears dangling expensive earrings.

The quick work of the burial crews prevented sickness from sweeping the city. And when, finally, the heartbreaking task of removing the dead was completed and the injured at last cared for, residents of Galveston took a long look at the rebuilding job ahead of them. There was disagreement on what should be done. Some said that Galveston should be moved to the mainland, that the island was too low and too exposed to build a city on. But more stubborn citizens insisted that the city would remain. In its first edition following the disaster, the *Galveston Daily News* sided with the determined element. It said: GALVESTON MUST RISE AGAIN.

And Galveston did. The city was rebuilt, more beautiful than ever, and the level of the city actually was raised by jacking up 2,146 buildings and pumping in sand sucked out of the Gulf. A giant seawall—17,593 feet long, 16 feet wide and 17 feet high—was erected to protect the town against any new disaster. That seawall was tested in 1915 when another major hurricane swept the coast. It did the job and the city survived.

Today, Galveston is again a thriving metropolis and a popular resort. The great hurricane of 1900—which killed more people than any other hurricane in American history—is a nightmare residents of the city prefer to forget. And they can take comfort now in the knowledge that their great seawall (since extended to 43,641 feet, or 8.26 miles) makes Galveston one of the best protected cities on any American coast.

5

Wild Wind from the West Indies

Florida (1928)

In the narrows of the South Atlantic—the 1,600-mile-wide "channel" between South America and Africa—two American freighters approached each other from opposite directions. One was the *Commack,* heading north toward Boston; the other the *Clearwater,* southward bound toward Rio de Janiero. About 250 miles separated the two ships.

Captain Leonard Watkins, in the wheelhouse of the *Commack,* scanned the evening sky with special interest. It had been a calm and clear day and the sun was now sinking behind the rim of water that marked the western horizon. But instead of the vivid orange coloring usually associated with the sun setting over a smooth blue-green sea, there was an obscure milky haze that seemed strange and unreal to the captain. He went to bed that night with troubled thoughts, and when he arose the next morning he checked the weather again. There was no visible sign of a storm in the area, yet the sky had now taken on an ominous brownish color. When

Captain Watkins discovered that his barometer was dropping a fifth-of-an-inch every two hours, he decided to contact other ships in the area. Before long he was talking to Captain A. O. Oden of the *Clearwater*. The two ships were by this time only 100 miles apart.

Comparing barometer readings and making other calculations, the two captains decided that, although the weather was clear with little wind in their specific areas, there was definitely a storm center nearby. Exactly where it was, and how serious it was, were questions that needed answering.

Both captains agreed to contact other ships in the South Atlantic in an attempt to pinpoint the exact location of the storm. Eventually they reached the *Erdine*, a British vessel, and the three ships' captains went into radio-conference. Immediately the story became clear. Each ship was feeling a light wind, but in each case the wind was coming from a different direction. That meant only one thing—a revolving turbulence that threatened to become a full-blown hurricane was brewing among them. The *Clearwater* was approaching the storm from the north, the *Commack* was on the east edge of it, and the *Erdine* was just to it's west.

After pooling the information, a radio communication was sent to the weather bureau in Washington, D. C., advising of an embryonic storm in the South Atlantic that might become a killer hurricane. How much of a killer neither the three ships' captains nor the weather bureau could guess. But this hurricane of September 1928 was to kill 600 people on the French island of Guadeloupe, 1,000 in Puerto Rico, and 2,000 in Florida. It would then rage up the eastern coast all the way to Maine, adding to its ghastly toll—eventually claiming a total of 4,000 lives in a ten-day rampage.

It was fortunate that at the moment the Washington weather bureau received the warning, a man named Charles L. Mitchell was on hand. Mitchell was an expert on West

Indies hurricanes. He had charted 300 of them meticulously and had learned not only the routes they normally took but the reasons for their occasional departures from the norm. With his maps, his charts, and his knowledge, Mitchell was able to determine the exact location of the hurricane stirring in the South Atlantic, estimate that it was traveling north at the rate of 450 miles each 24 hours, and radio warnings to those inhabited areas along its expected path 24 to 60 hours in advance.

Mitchell's prediction of the hurricane's course, as he sat 3,000 miles away in his Washington office, was one of the most brilliant in weather bureau history. No hurricane had been so closely tracked or its potential so carefully analyzed. Mitchell's accurate forecasting made it possible for all ships at sea to avoid the storm; he foretold which Caribbean islands would be hit by the storm and which would be spared; he advised the people of the threatened islands exactly when they could expect the hurricane's arrival; and he warned Floridians 16 hours in advance that the blow would strike their peninsula and pinpointed the exact spot where it would storm ashore. How many lives this man saved will never be known, but certainly thousands more would have perished in the raging winds and torrential rains had not Mitchell worked ceaselessly for a week, charting the course of what became one of the most devastating hurricanes ever to batter the Caribbean islands and the coastal areas of the United States.

The hurricane struck Puerto Rico—an island only two-thirds the size of Connecticut with a population of 1,400,000—on the morning of September 13. It raged all day and far into the night with the winds reaching 132 miles an hour in mid-afternoon before it carried away the weather bureau anemometer at San Juan. For six of the long hours of agony the winds remained at 100 miles an hour.

The vicious storm had already swept over the French-held

island of Guadeloupe in the Leeward chain, inflicting 600 deaths, 27 of them in the town of Bourg where a tidal wave thundered ashore. At St. Croix and St. Thomas, in the Virgin Islands group, homes, sugar factories and crops were destroyed, and 50 more met death; on the British islands of Nevis, Montserrat and St. Kitts, the storm claimed additional victims. Now it was battering Puerto Rico, ravaging both cities and farmland as it roared across the stricken island.

In San Juan, Puerto Rico's principal city, the tempest flattened hundreds of homes and partially destroyed hundreds more. The roof of the Hotel Palace in the heart of the city was carried off by the wind, and the Union Club was decapitated in the same manner. In port, the freighter *Helen*, battered savagely by the winds, pulled her anchor and drifted onto rocks in the harbor area. Two other vessels in the harbor went to the bottom. Windows and doors were blown off the Governor's Palace and the building was flooded by the heavy rains. Twenty large school buildings crumpled under the onslaught and an estimated 1,000 one- and two-room schools were leveled. By mid-afternoon all telegraph and telephone communication between San Juan and other cities was severed.

The Puerto Rican passenger liner *San Lorenzo* rode out the storm at dockside. For 36 hours she was mauled by the wind and rain, but unlike smaller craft that were completely destroyed by the big blow the ocean liner managed to stay afloat. From Stella Rice, an American aboard the ship, came one of the best eye-witness accounts of the calamity:

> It was [she said] almost like watching a movie or a play. One had a detached, lonesome sense of seeing something happen without being a part of it. All the time there was the tremendous roar that made any conversation impossible. Passengers were kept away from portholes and windows, so we could see but a tiny section of the storm as though at a distance. Vision, anyway, was limited to a few feet in the grayness. We could see

whole houses hurtle by and tall trees swept along by the wind. Occasionally fishing smacks would bob past and go crashing up on the beach. For a little while there was a lull and then the hurricane raced up to 100 miles an hour. The rain came down as though we were directly beneath Niagara Falls. The decks ran deep in water. We knew it only afterward, but a great ammonia plant only a few hundred feet from us blew up during the storm.

Before the horrid day and night were over, 1,000 people were dead. Half the island's citizens were homeless, 300,000 in San Juan alone. The city of San Juan was badly damaged, with many buildings totally destroyed, and small towns all across the island were wiped out.

But perhaps the hardest blow for the agriculture-oriented Puerto Ricans was the almost complete loss of crops. The sugarcane harvest, which by the middle of August had been particularly promising, was reduced by some 200,000 short tons. Grapefruit and oranges were blown from trees, 90 per cent of the coffee industry was destroyed, and minor crops of bananas and rice were completely ruined. Suddenly Puerto Ricans found themselves not only without means of livelihood, but without food.

Personal tragedies occurred all over the island. Felicia Cartegena, a telephone operator at the little town of Coamo, sat at her switchboard calmly sending out warnings and asking for aid as the great storm swirled around. Suddenly the roof collapsed and she was killed. One mother at Cayey was found with a child in each arm, all three almost cut in two by a flying sheet of roofing. In the same city a merchant admitted a man to his store who was seeking shelter. Before the merchant could close the door against the howling winds he was blown into the river and drowned. At Guayama fourteen people sought protection in a partially-constructed church, but all were lost when the building crumbled on top of them. At Guarderraya a freakish trick of the wind collapsed a public school but left the blackboards standing with spelling lessons of the day chalked in large letters.

The aftermath was as bad as the storm itself. Hungry people roamed the countryside. Refugees from outlying areas poured into San Juan by the thousands, although the city was unable for some time to help them. Hard-pressed merchants generously passed out what food they had left. At Naguabo Playa, hungry and homeless victims of the storm attacked an old man who had a bag of beans, a bag of rice, and a side of pork, tearing the food from him and eating it like famished wolves.

Before help could come from the American Red Cross and the United States government, food riots erupted in San Juan, and both influenza and malaria swept the island.

As the hurricane hurtled past Puerto Rico and moved in a northwesterly direction past the Dominican Republic toward the Bahama Islands and the coast of Florida, weather forecaster Charles Mitchell in Washington was faced with a critical decision. Aware of the habits of West Indies hurricanes, Mitchell knew that there were now two possible routes for the big storm. It would either maintain its present course, in which case it would strike the Florida coastline, or it would veer to the north and blow itself out at sea. Mitchell did not want to alarm Florida residents unnecessarily if the hurricane were fated to shift away from the state's east coast. Neither did he want to sooth them with false information that the storm was headed up the Atlantic; such a forecast, if proven wrong, could cost thousands of lives.

It was early Sunday morning, September 16. Mitchell was studying his charts and maps when he was suddenly caught up short by one important factor in his readings. Far to the north in the Atlantic Ocean, off the coast of Canada, was an area of "low barometer." This low, he knew, was significant. Such lows act as a barrier to hurricanes. Mitchell knew at once that the low—as far away as it was—would prevent the storm from turning north. That meant that it would keep on its present course, hitting Florida with all the savagery it had built up in its long journey from the South Atlantic.

Storm warnings were already up in Florida, but there had been no preparations made to meet anything but a fairly severe blow. Now Mitchell used the phrase "hurricane warning" for the first time. By close attention to his data, he even predicted where the brunt of the storm would hit. It would smash ashore between the tiny town of Jupiter and the two Palm Beaches. Mitchell's forecast read this way:

"Hoist hurricane warnings 10:30 A.M. Miami to Daytona, Florida. Northeast storm warnings displayed north of Daytona to Savannah and northwest storm warnings south of Miami to Key West and north of Key West to Punta Gorda. . . . Indications are that hurricane center will reach the Florida coast near Jupiter early tonight. Emergency. Advise all interests. This hurricane is of wide extent and great severity. Every precaution should be taken against destructive winds and high tides on Florida east coast, especially West Palm Beach to Daytona."

People responded. They remembered a similar storm that had devastated Miami two years earlier, and they promptly boarded up windows in their homes and took shelter in stronger public buildings.

Palm Beach proper was, and is today, the most exclusive of the Florida winter resorts. It derives its name from the spectacular palm trees that stretch for miles along the beach in each direction, and it boasts the most luxurious private homes and hotels along the eastern coast. It is a playground for celebrities and millionaires who bask on the sun-splashed beaches, ride the bridle paths that wind through tropical foliage, and walk or drive along the wide boulevards.

West Palm Beach is the business center, with stores, banks, newspaper offices and other commercial activities that draw patronage from both communities.

The hurricane stormed ashore at 5:50 P.M. on September

16 with winds reaching 125 miles an hour. It hit precisely where Mitchell predicted, in the Jupiter-Palm Beach area. Under a triple attack of high winds, torrential rains and raging seas, homes both in West Palm Beach and Palm Beach proper suffered heavy damage. More solidly built structures, such as hotels and business offices, trembled but stood up.

For two hours the hurricane did its worst. Wires were down throughout the Palm Beach area, cutting off communication with more fortunate towns. Expensive yachts were battered to pieces by the howling wind. Palatial homes in the exclusive North Ocean Boulevard section were ravaged, including the home of Mrs. Hugh Dillman, widow of the automobile titan Horace Dodge, and the Harold Vanderbilt residence.

Smaller cottages were particularly vulnerable. Either they collapsed under the onslaught or lost their roofs to the driving gale. Throughout the Palm Beaches, and for miles around, statuesque palm trees were uprooted. Coconuts were ripped from the trees and hurled like cannon balls through the air. Most of the stores in the business district of West Palm Beach were smashed, and the American Legion's open-air arena was leveled.

Walter Chamblin, an Associated Press staff writer, traveled through the Palm Beach area two days after the blow on a train and described the destruction this way:

> Two out of every three buildings in the business district of West Palm Beach [he wrote] are wrecked or damaged. The big hotels at Palm Beach apparently escaped without serious injury, but a part of the Royal Palm Hotel was under four feet of water swept up from the ocean. As our train progressed, the scenes of wreckage came more frequently. Lumber mills, a furniture warehouse, homes and other structures were wrecked by the dozens. Seventeen box cars were blown over on the east coast tracks between Bluefield and West Palm Beach.

Cities on the fringe of the storm were rocked by strong

winds, but with less severe results—small yachts smashed in the Halifax River at Daytona Beach to the north, slight damage to homes in Fort Lauderdale to the south, and docks crumpled and a radio tower down in Jupiter. But most important of all was the fact that Mitchell's early warnings had dramatically reduced the death toll along the coast. Unlike the experience at Galveston, where people had received little warning and refused even to believe what they heard, Florida residents took cover in large buildings, where most escaped the storm's wrath.

But one major tragedy occurred in inland Florida that neither Mitchell nor anyone else could possibly have predicted. In the Everglades country some 40 miles due west of the Palm Beaches lay Lake Okeechobee—one of the largest lakes entirely within the boundaries of a single state, and one that was to prove defenseless against the destructive wind and rain of the hurricane. Circular in shape and shallow in depth, Okeechobee rarely showed an angry ripple on its serene surface. Nevertheless, because of frequent overflows, it was flanked by dikes and drainage canals that kept its waters from spilling into the swampy basin to the south that harbored such towns as Belle Glade, South Bay and Pelican Bay.

The Okeechobee region was considered one of the best farming areas in the country, and 1928 had been a banner year. September was the month for winter plantings of vegetables, and most farmers were busy at the task when the hurricane threatened the region. Tractors prowled up and down the fields, plowing the moist soil for the new plantings. Some 5,000 itinerant laborers, who lived in jerry-built shacks and tents in the lowlands, worked in the fields. No one gave much thought to placid Lake Okeechobee, which actually lay above the level of most of the farms.

During August and early September an unusual amount of rain had pelted the area, filling the canals and raising the water in the lake almost to the crest of the dikes. These were made of mucky earth rather than cement, and even though they held, knowledgeable old-timers allowed as how the "levees might spring a leak here and there."

The Everglades people had little warning that disaster was imminent. Very few farmers had either radios or telephones, and most of them were completely unaware of the hurricane roaring up from the West Indies. It was not until noon of the evening the hurricane hit that business men and government authorities in the tiny towns learned that they were in the path of a serious blow. Immediately they set out in cars to warn the farmers and their families. Business men from South Bay roamed the country south of Lake Okeechobee, picking up more than 200 people and transferring them to a huge barge on the lake. Other men left Belle Glade, calling on farmers and inducing them to abandon their vulnerable homes and take refuge in the city. By mid-afternoon, with the winds of the storm already battering the area, some 500 men, women and children were quartered at two hotels in Belle Glade. Unfortunately, however, some farmers refused to leave their homes, preferring to ride out the hurricane on familiar ground.

By early evening the winds of the tempest, plowing out of the north, were at their highest velocity. In the cities of Belle Glade, South Bay and Pelican Bay trees were uprooted and hurled against homes and barns; automobiles were over-turned; roofs were ripped from houses, traveling through the air like huge flying carpets; buildings were leveled and farm wagons picked up and carried away by the powerful gale.

But this was only a prelude. The heavy rain now added a new dimension to the storm, quickly filling Lake Okeecho-bee to its brim. The wind out of the north was so powerful that it pushed tons of lake water to the south, almost blowing the northern half of Lake Okeechobee dry. Unable to with-stand the pressure of wind and water, the dikes along the southern perimeter of the lake crumbled, and a wall of water eight feet high bore down on the swampy farmlands. In a matter of minutes, homes were swept away and people drowned in the flood.

Belle Glade was directly in the path of the towering wall of water. It hit the town with thunderous impact, crushing houses or picking them up on the crest of the wave and carrying them into the flatlands. It tore up telephone poles and hurled them through the air like spears, felled huge trees, and smashed commercial buildings like eggshells. Those who had refused to seek safety in the two hotels were drowned in the streets, and for many anxious moments even the hotels teetered on the edge of disintegration. One of them, trembling under the force of the wave, was moved off its foundations but remained standing. In the other, people were forced to move up to the second floor as water surged into the lobby.

In South Bay, building after building was flattened, but the 200 people who had sought safety on the barge survived. Pelican Bay's inhabitants were not as lucky. Just before the wall of water emerged, the population of 900 people split in half on a crucial decision. One group of people decided to stay in their homes; the other set out on foot toward Belle Glade, where they thought they would be safer. Both groups perished to the man. Those who stayed in their homes were killed by the winds or drowned; those on the road to Belle Glade were caught in the open and washed away to watery deaths.

L. A. Hargraves, a farmer near Belle Glade, survived the murderous winds. His tiny house began to creak and groan as the hurricane tore it apart. Knowing that it would collapse in minutes, he raced outside to a neighbor's home that seemed more substantial. To his dismay he found that this house, too, was on the verge of crumbling. Eventually he reached a third home where twelve other men were holed up. This house withstood the wind for half an hour before it showed signs of collapsing. In the sparsely settled region,

Hargraves could not find other shelter. He crawled aimlessly on his hands and knees, afraid to stand up for fear the raging winds would carry him away. After traveling a quarter of a mile in this fashion, he saw a massive tree ahead of him. Water from the broken dike was now beginning to roll over the area and Hargraves climbed into the tree. To his surprise he found a man and his wife clinging to the topmost branch.

The watery blitzkrieg attacked the tree with all its force and, although water around the tree rose nine feet in 30 minutes, the tree continued to stand. Later Hargraves said, "While I was in the tree I saw the house with the twelve men washed away. I never saw the occupants of the house again." Hargraves and the couple were rescued from their perilous perch the next morning.

D. H. Walker, a farmer, was one of the lucky ones who escaped the sudden flood. His house, just outside of South Bay, was not engulfed by the great wave of water coming from the broken dikes. He, his wife and five children, managed to reach a houseboat, along with more than 50 others. A few minutes later his home was swept away. "I saw a lot of people, unable to reach the houseboat, floating along clinging to driftwood," he said. "Practically all the territory in that section was suddenly under water."

Some people were actually caught on the surface of Lake Okeechobee during the seige of wind and water—and some even lived through the ordeal. On Torrey Island, 21 men were working in a packing house. When water rushed through the building they climbed into the rafters to escape. But the wild waters were too much for the structure and it finally crumbled. Nine men were swept to their deaths; twelve miraculously escaped.

C. E. Thomas and his wife and six children were trapped in their home on Ritta Island. Water first seeped slowly into the ground floor of their home, and as huge waves pounded the house the room began to fill with water. Frantically, the family took refuge in the attic. While they huddled in their precarious shelter, a huge tree uprooted by the waves shattered the house like a battering ram, and the family was tossed into the flood waters. The following day Thomas was rescued by a boat, but the bodies of his family were recovered later, miles away from their island home.

Thelma Martin, a twelve-year-old girl, became a heroine. When flood waters tore her home apart, Thelma quickly grabbed her seven-year-old sister, Ernestine, and two-year-old brother, Aaron, as the waters bore them away at lightning speed. Thelma managed to cling to a log until they became lodged against a banyan tree. Pinned there by the log and other debris, Thelma was able to hold Aaron's head above water to keep him from drowning. The next morning the three youngsters were rescued.

Many of those who survived the great wall of water spent a terrifying night. Poisonous snakes, disgorged from the swamplands by the thousands, were a particular menace. Frightened and with an instinct to strike at anything near, the snakes claimed a number of lives. One man who had managed to scurry with his young son to a hummock of high ground fought off snakes all night, kicking them aside with his boots and holding the boy out of their reach. But he was bitten repeatedly and finally fell unconscious. The snakes writhed over the man and his son, and both were found dead the next morning.

By the time the winds finally lapsed and the flood waters abated, 2,000 people had perished. No one—not even Mitchell—had expected anything more troublesome than heavy winds in the Okeechobee area; they had not foreseen the collapse of the lake's flimsy dikes.

The worst was over, but conditions in the Lake Okeechobee region after the storm passed remained critical. More than 8,000 people were in need of food, clothing and medical aid. Some, who stood in waist-deep water for hours, had contracted pneumonia. Tom A. Pledge, an Associated Press reporter, reached South Bay after the storm had blown over. He counted 41 bodies lying in a field near the center of town and asked a relief worker what would be done with them. "When we can get enough men to round up the dead and pile them up, we'll burn them," he said simply.

Pledge found that 544 people out of a population of 700 were missing at South Bay and that the town itself was in complete ruin. He went on to Belle Glade, where he reported that "conditions beggared description. No building in the town remained undamaged. Only three in the business district were inhabitable. Hundreds of homeless refugees from outlying districts paraded up and down the street, aimlessly moving from place to place. Hundreds of crude unpainted coffins cluttered the streets. Trucks came and went bringing loads of coffins and then taking out the dead."

Rescue and rehabilitation efforts got under way. The American Legion, the Red Cross, Coast Guard, National Guard, state and local officials and ordinary citizens accomplished miracles. In less than a week these agencies established feeding stations for nearly 15,000 people in the devastated Lake Okeechobee region. In Puerto Rico, health authorities struggled with 2,000 injuries, 15,000 cases of influenza and 5,000 cases of malaria; in the Virgin Islands, 15,000 homeless people were cared for and fed. In time, ravaged towns in the Caribbean and Florida were cleaned up and, where necessary, rebuilt.

Looking back on the unimaginable destruction, the *Detroit Free Press,* from its insulated position in the midwest, took a fatalistic but nevertheless true view of the tragic hurricane. It stated, "Tropical storms are to Florida what earthquakes are to parts of California and tornadoes to sections of the middle west. Their effect on real estate values is less than it would be if there were not plenty of people willing to tempt fate by crossing their paths. As long as man sets up roofs for hurricanes to send hurtling through the air there will be a reason for the American Red Cross—and also a reason for the public to meet its appeals for funds promptly and generously.''

Total deaths—including those in Guadeloupe, the Virgin Islands, Puerto Rico and Florida—numbered 4,000. Property damage reached $30,000,000 in Palm Beach County and $100,000,000 in Puerto Rico. The storm itself raced up to Cape Hatteras, South Carolina, before losing its steam, but its impact was felt as far north as Maine. The storm lasted ten days and ten nights, during which Charles Mitchell mapped it every inch of the way. When it finally ended, the Washington weather bureau issued a report that was perhaps the understatement of the decade: ''Few West Indies hurricanes have been so severe as this one for so long a time.''

Few, indeed.

6

The Storm That Lost Its Way

New England (1938)

It was September 1938. The world teetered on the brink of war. Reichsfuehrer Adolf Hitler was rattling the saber in Europe, boasting of German might and threatening Czechoslovakia. Neville Chamberlain, prime minister of England, was preparing to make his ill-fated journey to Munich, seeking "peace in our time."

Day after day American newspapers ran front page stories detailing the ominous steps being taken toward world catastrophe. In this atmosphere it is little wonder that a hurricane brewing in the Caribbean received little notice. A windstorm seemed only a minor annoyance when the world was about to go up in flames.

It was on September 18 that the *New York Times* first recognized the existence of the Caribbean storm, grudgingly allotting three inches of space to the news. The story simply announced that a hurricane hovered over the Atlantic Ocean about 450 miles north of San Juan and 900 miles east-southeast of Miami, moving at 20 miles an hour. It contained a brief bulletin that said, "Caution advised, all vessels in path and all small craft, Cape Hatteras to Florida Straits, should remain in port until storm passes." That was all.

Floridians, accustomed to storms out of the West Indies, were more hurricane-conscious than the northerners who read the *New York Times*. They automatically boarded up windows and took other precautions to face the storm should it strike their east coast. But the next day, September 19, they were assured by Grady Norton of the Jacksonville Weather Bureau that the storm had this time bypassed the Florida peninsula and had veered out to sea.

In providing Florida with the "all clear" signal, however, Norton made a prophetic statement. He said it was "impossible to say that the entire Atlantic coast would escape damage." New England forecasters, apparently, either ignored this plain warning or gave it little credence. After all, the New England states were not located in hurricane country. Occasionally they might be sideswiped by peripheral winds as some hurricane roared out to sea, but these were rarely dangerous or destructive. They saw no reason why this storm should not follow the familiar path.

Had New York City's weather bureau or other forecasters in the North been more alert, they would have noticed a set of freakish atmospheric conditions indicating that the hurricane was on a collision course with Long Island and the New England states. A bank of warm air lay over the ocean to the east. To the west a similar bank of cold air lay dormant. These two ridges of air formed a perfect trough for the hurricane winds moving northward. That trough indicated that the great wind from the south would brush the New Jersey coast, break in all its fury on Long Island, and race northward into New England.

The comfortable feeling that hurricanes were tropical phenomena that never touched New England was evident among northeasterners even on September 20 when the storm was becoming more menacing. Weather bureaus throughout the area failed to warn citizens of the extent and power of the blow approaching them until it was too late to take adequate cover. The *New York Times* admitted that the tropical storm would hit the Jersey coast but thought so little of its potential that it ran the article on page 27!

Even when the hurricane sideswiped the New Jersey coast, no particular warning was issued by northeast weather bureaus. Forecasters seemed confident that the storm would veer northeast and blow itself out over the Atlantic, when in reality it was headed for a frontal attack on the southern shore of Long Island.

Although the coast of New Jersey suffered some damage, it was nothing like the devastation eventually visited on Long Island. Jersey City, Newark, Paterson and other large towns had electric and telephone service disrupted, shingles lifted from homes, chimneys toppled, and plate glass windows broken. Large trees were felled and trolley lines downed, and in the countryside the tomato and apple crops were damaged.

The shoreline suffered when a succession of tidal waves rolled in from the sea. Miles of boardwalks at Atlantic City, Asbury Park and other resort areas were torn up and carried inland, a bridge connecting Atlantic City and Brigantine Island collapsed, and a number of seaside cottages were overturned. In one case a man standing on a bulkhead near his ocean-side cottage, which was normally ten feet above high tide, was swept away by a tidal wave. When the wave receded it carried him back and deposited him on the bulkhead again. He was unhurt, but his wife, who saw it happen, was taken to a hospital suffering from shock.

The damage to New Jersey from peripheral winds left New York and New England weather bureaus unimpressed. In fact, it was not until the afternoon of September 21, when the outside rim of the revolving hurricane was already buffeting Long Island's exposed shoreline, that the New York City weather bureau suddenly realized that the storm was going to strike inland with great fury. At 3 P.M. they issued a hasty but somewhat bland bulletin advising that the storm (they were reluctant to call it a hurricane) would pass over Long Island and Connecticut "late this afternoon or tonight, attended by shifting gales."

The tardiness of this report left small coastal towns, fishing villages, and cottage-dwellers along the beaches completely unprepared for the hurricane. The approaching storm and the human failure to evaluate and properly report it had set the stage for disaster.

The raging torrent of rain and wind struck the south shore of Long Island precisely at its center, bringing almost instant calamity to the entire banana-shaped spit of land. From Montauk at its eastern tip to Queens and Brooklyn at its western terminus, the island was reduced to mangled wreckage.

Huge waves churned up by the winds—some 30 to 40 feet high—smashed across the shoreline. Cottages along the beach crumbled under the onslaught, roads were submerged by several feet of water, and massive trees were uprooted, crashing down on homes and blocking highways. Electric service was disrupted and the island was plunged into an eerie afternoon darkness; telephone poles fell and live wires spit and hissed on the wet streets. Small craft all along the coast were torn from their moorings and carried ashore by the rampaging seas.

The Hamptons—a series of five glamorous resorts spaced along 30 miles of sandy shoreline—were directly in the hurricane's path. Westhampton Beach, the most fashionable seashore colony, was devastated. Fifty substantially-built summer homes—some boasting 30 rooms—were washed out to sea. In one case, seventeen frightened people took refuge on the second floor of a well-built mansion, where they huddled chest-deep in water until the walls of the building crumbled and all were drowned. The sandy beaches were deeply channeled and lawns a mile inland were ruined by the invading sea. Monster waves flooded the main section of the town to a depth of eight feet and winds flattened buildings, turning the entire area into a shambles.

Southampton, another plush resort, suffered similar destruction, with homes torn apart by the winds or flooded by sea water, and its luxurious Beach Club completely demolished. There was comparable damage in East Hampton, where the wind and pounding seas swept 100 cabanas of the Maidstone Club into the ocean, flooded the main clubhouse and inundated the golf course, then went on to tear off the roof of the Maidstone Hotel, largest hostelry in the area. In Beach Hampton, houses were destroyed and the plush Barbour Restaurant was reduced to ruins; at Long Beach a hospital was flooded and cottages along the water blown down; in Patchogue the clubhouse of the Belle Port Yacht Club was leveled and several 100-year-old trees uprooted; Bluepoint and Bayville were flooded and plagued by fallen trees and wires; 25 homes in Oak Beach were washed away; the Long Island Lighting Company's No. 2 plant at Hampstead Harbor was hit by a tidal wave and knocked out of service; at Atlantic Beach seven beach clubs, their cabanas and boardwalks were demolished; and at Port Washington 400 vessels ranging in size from rowboats to 70-foot yachts were torn loose from dockside and tossed on shore or blown out to the Sound.

Fire Island, a popular resort area for the less well-to-do, was almost entirely destroyed. The ocean broke through at Baltaire and poured across the island into Great South Bay. Of 100 cottages in its path, it left only 25 standing. The rest either caved in or were carried into the bay. A Rotary Club Center in Fire Island State Park—incongruously called

Camp Cheerful—was mutilated: twenty buildings wrecked. And amusement facilities at the same park—refreshment stands, bathhouses, a pavilion and boardwalk—were virtually pulverized.

Heightening the overall tragedy was the fact that the Coast Guard's rescue efforts were seriously hampered by the storm. Several Coast Guard stations were smashed to bits by giant waves. The Fire Island station went first, then the Jones Beach station, and finally several others located among the hard-hit Hamptons.

In its wild passage across the narrow peninsula of Long Island, the tempest played freakish pranks. A cabin cruiser was torn from its moorings and deposited on a golf course one-quarter of a mile inland. A man at Inwood was working on top of a 60-foot oil tank when the storm hit; he was killed when the wind lifted him from the tank and hurled him a hundred feet to his death. Three men in a small sailboat were caught by the wind and blown overboard; two of the men managed to swim ashore, towing the third along, but when they pulled him up on the beach they found the man they had "saved" was dead. At Greenport, 60 patrons of a movie theater miraculously escaped death when the winds blew the roof off the building, leaving them exposed to the rain but otherwise uninjured.

Mrs. Margaret Delehanty, an elderly woman residing at Point Lookout, east of Long Beach, became panic-stricken when huge waves smashed repeatedly at her beachside home. Her husband managed to get her into the family car and made a hazardous crossing of the Point Lookout causeway to take her to her doctor in Freeport. Just as the couple reached the office, Mrs. Delehanty fell dead, the victim of a heart attack.

In Port Washington Harbor, on the north shore of Long Island, Mrs. Peter Kelly was caught in a small schooner when the storm broke. She threw three anchors overboard, but they could not hold the boat against the whistling winds. Finally she tied a rope around the neck of her small terrier, who swam ashore with it. Men on shore took the rope and managed to pull the schooner in.

At the same harbor the Port Washington-to-New Rochelle ferryboat *Reliance* found that it could not be relied on to make its scheduled trip across the storm-whipped waters. As it lay at the dock, a tidal wave suddenly lifted it on high, tossing it aside, like a broken toy, onto a hill ten feet above the pier.

A children's party was in progress at the home of Mrs. Nevin Greene near Moriches Bay. The merriment of the nine adults and seven children ended abruptly as the storm struck. Within minutes the house was flooded and all fled to the attic. Fearing that the water would rise even higher, the men chopped a hole in the ceiling and, as the water came up, the sixteen party-goers climbed out and clung to the slanted roof. To their horror, a large section of the house broke away and carried them into Moriches Bay. It was a miracle that the house held together as it drifted for three miles in the turbulent waters. Near the coastline the under-structure collapsed and the roof was carried toward shore by the wind. It was beached on a sandy section of the shoreline, and all members of the party were rescued.

One of the most remarkable experiences was that of Countess Charles de Ferry de Fontnouvelle, wife of the French Consul General in New York. She, her 22-month-old daughter, a cook and the baby's governess, Agnes Zeigler, were at home in Westhampton Beach when the storm struck.

"The whole house started to tremble," said the Countess. "We knew something terrible was going to happen. The wind was howling and the water was up to the floor of the living room. I was never so frightened in my life. Miss Ziegler said she would try to find help. She went out but was unable to find anyone. So when she returned I bundled the baby in a blanket and we all started out together—Miss Ziegler, the baby, the cook and myself.

"Water swirled around our hips. Planks, branches and all sorts of thing were flying through the air. It was only by the grace of God that we were not killed."

Battling rain, wind and flying debris, the four refugees made their painful way up the beach, hoping to reach another home a half mile away. At one point they heard a thunderous crash behind them and turned to see the house they had left collapse. Finally they reached the seaside home of William Ottman, Jr. But the Ottman house was endangered also, and the group spent seven hours of terror in the shaking home.

"The hero of everything was the Ottman butler," the Countess said. "I wish I knew the name of that brave man. He quieted everybody when the storm was at its worst."

At one point the butler went to the roof and attempted to signal for help with a flashlight. There was an answering light off in the distance, but no help came.

Shortly before midnight the butler, who had left the building, returned with three husky young boys. With their help, the group linked arms and battled their way through the storm to a more sheltered area inland. They had gone only a short distance when the Ottman home was swept out to sea. The Countess and her party were finally taken into the home of John O'Conner, where they survived the rest of the storm.

Anna Hampton, her husband and her mother, were in their seaside home when a wall of water struck. "It came so suddenly," Mrs. Hampton said, "that I didn't realize what was happening. We were carried right out of the house by the water and started swimming. I looked around and my mother was gone. My husband and I kept on swimming and finally got to shore." Mrs. Hampton's mother was never found.

Mrs. George McKnight, whose husband was in New York

City on business, spent a terrifying night in her home close to the beach. Certain that her house would collapse at any moment, she saw no hope of survival. Sadly, she wrote a note of farewell to her husband and nailed it to a rafter, hoping it would eventually be found. But the house stood up and she was rescued the next morning.

David Potts was cruising in Moriches Bay in his 32-foot cruiser *Dorel* and decided to ride out the storm. He fought the angry winds and horrendous waves for hours, the cruiser bobbing around like a rowboat. Finally he decided to put down an anchor in the hope of steadying the craft. When the storm ended and the heavy seas receded, he found he had dropped anchor on someone's front lawn.

While utter destruction was the lot of Long Island, the City of New York and its environs escaped the full force of the hurricane. The heavily populated areas of Manhattan, Brooklyn, Queens and the Bronx were battered by winds that reached a peak of 75 miles an hour—enough to qualify the storm as a hurricane even though the New York City Weather Bureau preferred to label it "whole gale force", explaining that 75-mile-an-hour winds had to be sustained for a period of time to qualify as a hurricane. In any case, damage was light compared to the devastation of Long Island.

During the height of the storm, commuter services to outlying areas were interrupted. Many office workers were marooned in business buildings in Manhattan and small craft on the waterfront were grounded. In Brooklyn, trolley lines were down and the city was plunged into darkness by damage to electric power lines. In the Bronx and Queens, cellars were flooded by the heavy downpour, streets and highways covered with water, and garages overturned by the wind.

Two great ocean liners were caught up in the storm. The Cunard White Star Line's *Queen Mary* was scheduled to sail for Europe at 4:30 P.M. Most of her passengers had already boarded when word came from the Coast Guard that the liner might encounter the center of the hurricane as she left her Hudson River wharfage and headed out to sea. As a result, the sailing time was rescheduled for 5 A.M. the next morning and those passengers who wanted to go ashore were permitted to do so. Most, however, preferred to wait out the storm on the palatial liner.

Meanwhile the French liner *Ile de France*, putting into New York, took heavy winds on her portside and was listing badly to starboard as she limped into New York. It took twelve tugs to bring her into port.

A much smaller ship—the Staten Island ferryboat *Knickerbocker*—threw 200 passengers into panic when she almost tipped over in her slip at the Battery. The storm-tossed waters picked the boat up and threw her against the dock where her port bow lodged under an iron railing, leaving the vessel tilted at a 45-degree angle. Passengers tumbled about like tenpins, screaming in terror as the boat remained at its perilous slant. Eventually two tugboats managed to pry the *Knickerbocker* loose.

While the hurricane was treating New Yorkers to a mild taste of its destructive powers, it was concentrating its full force on the New England states. Having virtually demolished Long Island, the center of the great storm moved north toward New England, doing particular damage to Connecticut, Rhode Island and Massachusetts. It attacked with screaming 100-mile-an-hour winds and torrential downpours. Streams and rivers, already swollen by a week of rains, flooded large areas of open country and raged through the streets of some cities. Many scenic college campuses were defaced. Age-old trees were torn up. Roofs blew away. Landslides blocked roads, barns crumbled and at least two dams burst.

Towering waves came in from the sea to flood coastal villages. Wires were down everywhere, and for a long time there was no communication between upper New England and areas to the south. But eventually fragmentary reports of casualties and damage trickled into the Boston office of The Associated Press—horror stories that sketched in a picture of total disaster.

Twenty-eight men missing along the Massachusetts coast . . . shoppers and theater patrons trapped in parked automobiles and forced to swim to safety . . . an eighteen-year-old girl crushed to death when a brick wall fell on top of her car . . . many killed as a seven-story building caved in . . . a woman drowned in several feet of water in the business section of a city . . . a man drowned when a wharf building in which he sought shelter plunged into the sea . . . a 55-year-old woman killed by a collapsing chimney . . . only one building out of thirty still standing in a town . . . hundreds driven from their homes by raging waters . . . four women swept to their deaths as a bridge caved in . . . four men drowned as a tugboat in a harbor sank . . . major operations performed at a hospital under emergency lighting . . . a man, blown through a plate glass window, falling 50 feet to the ground . . . and on and on.

Providence, Rhode Island, was among several major cities hard-hit by the tempest. The city was plunged at once into darkness, and communications with other parts of the country severed. Homes and buildings shuddered before the vicious winds; some losing their roofs while others were torn completely apart. Then, at 4 P.M. came the *coupe de grace* in the form of a huge tidal wave that raced directly into the heart of the city.

It came with no warning. Most of the people in the business district had already taken shelter from the heavy rain, but some were walking the streets in raincoats and many more huddled in automobiles. Suddenly the waters of Narragansett Bay were picked up by the hurricane and hurled with tremendous force into the city. Automobiles at the curbs were flooded, drowning people inside of them. Other cars were overturned by the force of the waters. Three hundred men, women and children were marooned for the night in the City Hall. Others were killed by falling walls weakened by the flood. Trees fell on moving automobiles, crushing drivers and passengers. Store fronts were damaged and plate glass windows shattered. Lobbies of hotels and ground floors of business buildings were swamped as the water suddenly rose to six feet. One man was drowned at the corner of Dorrance and Westminster Street, the very center of town. Before the wave finally subsided, the water depth reached twelve feet, forcing people to rush to the second floor of business and department store buildings to escape. Altogether, the flood marooned an estimated 15,000 people who huddled in storm-swept buildings all night.

L. D. Lacy, a visitor to Providence, gave an interesting description of the hurricane's fury. "I was standing in the main waiting room of the Union Station in Providence," he related. "I was waiting for trains which never came, when the principal arch over the room began to give way under the pressure of rain and wind. As the first piece of glass broke away from the frames above, the crowd below scurried for shelter, but many were cut by flying fragments. In a few moments the glass came down in a shower and as the arch started to crumble it ripped the metal roofing away. But fortunately the roofing remained intact."

Lacy, along with other would-be train passengers, ran from the station and took refuge in the Biltmore Hotel nearby. Water from the heavy rains was two inches deep in the street at the time, but the tidal wave had not yet hit the city. Lacy went on:

> As we reached the second floor lobby of the hotel [he said] it seemed as though we were comparatively safe, but we had not taken into consideration what amounted to an impending tidal wave from Narragansett Bay. Within an hour the water in the

street had risen as high as the second story but did not quite reach the lobby.

Stores, banks and other places of business on the main level were flooded, debris was floating by in great masses and it seemed that the entire downtown area was doomed. We had reports that Narragansett Pier and the Yacht Club were wrecked but could not verify them. Then the water seemed to recede with the tide almost as swiftly as it had risen. The resulting damage was shocking. Almost at once the National Guard was called out to police the city and prevent looting. All power was shut off and there were no means of communication. Trains, busses, airplanes, taxis and all other modes of transportation were unavailable. Roads were washed out, wires down, air fields flooded and main highways were undermined or blocked by fallen trees and poles.

Van Wyck Mason, the noted novelist, was also caught in the hurricane. He had scheduled a trip to New York City to deliver a new manuscript to his publishers. Before he arrived there he had several narrow escapes from death and went through an ordeal at Providence during the height of the storm's fury. Mason left Nantucket by steamboat and had no difficulty until he passed Martha's Vineyard. At that point the wind velocity had increased noticeably, causing the boat to miss the New Bedford pier and smash into another. At New Bedford, Mason found that all planes were grounded, and that it would be necessary to take a bus as far as Providence.

Several frightening incidents happened during the bus ride. First a live wire fell on the bus, the spitting end of it luckily missing the metal roof. Then two heavy trees fell directly in front of the bus, causing the driver to make jarring stops. A little farther on, the bus got into water up to its running boards and was stalled for some time. Finally, as it approached Providence, with the wind howling ferociously and the rain splashing down, trees began to crash all around it. By some miracle the bus at last reached the Providence station intact.

But Mason's ordeal was not over. As he stepped out of the bus, a shower of bricks from a crumbled chimney fell almost at his feet. Next he saw an overturned car with a woman inside and stopped to free her. In a hurry to get to New York for his appointment, he rushed to the railroad station, arriving just in time to see the entire roof of the station blow away. Mason stood in the rain-slashed station and watched in amazement as the water rose in the streets outside.

While he was watching he saw a woman who had taken refuge on top of her car plucked from the vehicle and drowned. "Another woman was wading to safety," he said, "when she popped out of sight just like a jack-in-the-box. She had evidently stepped into an open sewer."

Mason later explained that during the height of the flood "the lights of automobiles under the water stayed on, giving an eerie glow. Then the horns of automobiles all over the city short-circuited and kept up a deafening din."

Mason finally found refuge at the exclusive Hope Club for men, where he sat up all night. "For the first time in the history of the club," he said, "women—refugees, of course— were admitted within the doors. The oldsters at the club didn't like it. They said no good would come of it."

Providence, however, was only a focal point of the storm. Almost all of the tiny state of Rhode Island was devastated by the hurricane. For more than three hours, raging waters lashed at the state's shoreline. Seaside cottages were smashed to bits and in some cases carried out to sea as the hurricane took a heavy toll of life in these exposed areas. In one case a woman and her son, leaving Narragansett Pier just as the storm broke, were sucked into the sea and drowned. Seven children met a watery death in a school bus on an island in Narragansett Bay. The town of Westerly, at the southern tip of the state, counted 29 people killed and 52 missing. The storm flooded the printing plant of the *Providence Evening Bulletin,* more than half a mile inland, and the paper had to be printed in Boston the following day. In one case the winds picked up a cottage on the west side of Narragansett Bay and moved it over to the east side; two women were swept into the sea during the horrendous ride, but one managed to hang on and survive. A fishing village on the southeast side of the state was completely submerged by a tidal wave that rose twenty feet over the breakwater bordering on the Atlantic Ocean. A row of summer cottages at Misquamicut on Long Island Sound—including one in which ten women were attending a church social—was tossed into the sea; some people managed to cling to floating wreckage until rescued, but others were drowned.

A large group of people near the town of Watch Hill climbed upon a high sand dune to escape the towering seas, but the waves caught them and took them to their deaths. One woman, underestimating the power of the sea, stood on a beach watching the massive waves. A wave threw her against a fallen telephone pole, entangling her in the wires, and she was held fast as the pole drifted out on Narragansett Bay. The pole traversed the width of the bay, and when rescuers finally untied the woman she was found to have suffered only a broken arm.

Forty-five lives were lost and much damage done at the famous resorts of Newport, at the mouth of the bay. Bailey's Beach, society's summer capital, was completely destroyed by the high surf. Unlike those on Long Island, the homes of the wealthy held out for the most part against the hurricane, but much damage was done to grounds around the homes and to famous Ocean Drive. At one point the seawall along the drive was uprooted and giant chunks of granite, some weighing 200 pounds, were thrown across the drive. Swimming facilities on Newport Beach and Viking Beach, both exclusive bathing resorts, were demolished. The hurricane played no favorites, ruining the homes both of ordinary fishermen and of such members of high society as John Jacob Astor III, Vincent Astor, and Cornelius Vanderbilt.

In total, more than 250 people were killed in Rhode Island and millions of dollars of damage done to property in the short time the hurricane took to travel across the state.

Connecticut, its neighbor, also took the brunt of the storm. Cutting a wide swath, the hurricane swept over New London, New Haven and Bridgeport, all near the coastline, and then into the interior, where it ravaged Hartford and many small villages. For four hours the winds and rain battered the state, felled trees and light poles, and raised the water levels of rivers to flood crest, in the process turning the entire southern shoreline into marshland.

In New London an uncontrollable fire added to the city's woes. In the harbor was the barkentine *Marcelas*, a training ship. The savage winds tore at her until she broke her moorings and was blown ashore, a stove in the galley overturning and setting the ship afire. Defying the rain, the fire leaped from the ship to nearby buildings. Before long, flames had destroyed an entire block along Back Street, the roar of the holocaust and the crumbling of buildings muting even the howling noise of the storm.

In Bridgeport and East Bridgeport, giant elms were blown down, blocking streets all over the city. Roofs were lifted from homes and the streets were converted into rivers. In one case the wind played a freakish trick, ripping the steeple from the First Unitarian Church, flipping it over, and driving it point-down into the sanctuary. Aboard the *Park City*, a ferryboat running between Bridgeport and Port Jefferson, Long Island, six passengers and nine crew members spent an unforgettable 21 hours on Long Island Sound during the worst of the storm. The 150-foot car-carrying vessel left Port Jefferson at 2 P.M.—shortly before the arrival of the hurricane—its bow pointed toward Bridgeport. Within an hour the ship was bouncing around dangerously in the storm-tossed waters of the Sound. Gale winds whistled through the ship's superstructure and hurled waves over the deck. Passengers—including a two-month-old baby—huddled in an enclosed lounge or in their automobiles.

Before long the incessant pounding by the wind caused the ship to list badly and it was discovered that three feet of water had seeped into her hold, killing the engines and stalling the generator. Captain Ray Dickerson gave an account of the ordeal, calling it "the longest night I can ever remember":

> When we started from the harbor [he said] I thought that only a southeasterly wind was blowing. After we got well out into the Sound the waves assumed tremendous proportions and I attempted to turn back shortly after we approached the Middle Ground Light. But at that moment the wind shifted and I knew it was futile to try to move, so I anchored.
>
> As the gale reached its height the ship started to drag anchor, and we had plenty of worries even though the ship was at no time in danger of going down. Our main worry was wondering just where we were going to be blown. The waves kept pounding the deck and the boat shipped plenty of water. I put the entire crew and one of the passengers to work on the pumps.

When the ship was eventually towed in, H. L. Fry, a passenger, voiced the feelings of all those aboard. "I never expected to get back alive," he told a reporter. "It was a harrowing night. The only thing that saved us was the anchor. The crew was magnificent. We prayed and prayed fervently."

Most of the damage to Connecticut occurred along the coastline, and the tiny town of Mystic was a prime example. Heavy waves battered the village and played havoc with homes on the beaches. Of fifty cottages near shore, five were completely destroyed and the others heavily damaged.

Carolyn Wilson, a Mystic resident who owned a cottage set back a hundred yards from the sea, was desperately trying to plug leaks in her windows and walls where the heavy rains had penetrated. Suddenly, to her amazement, she saw the sea right at her door. She sought to leave the cottage but her cat refused to go, so she escaped alone by swimming a half mile past several water-filled beach homes to a less-battered house, where she was taken in.

Y. E. Soderberg, another Mystic resident, invited a host of people into his home, thinking it safe, but then discovered that water was rising inside the house. The group climbed to the second story and watched helplessly as first floor furniture floated away through broken windows.

The determined hurricane galloped across Connecticut into Massachusetts to repeat its devastating performance. It wrecked much of the farm country, but Boston, the capital city, was only lightly damaged. Although wind velocity in Boston reached 100 miles an hour, it retained that speed for only one minute, then slackened somewhat. Nevertheless, the winds were sufficient to make a confused shambles of Boston Harbor, splintering small craft and destroying docks.

By the following morning the hurricane had either crossed or sideswiped each of the New England states, treating some to extensive damage and only teasing others. By the time it blew into Canada, it had largely spent itself. In its wake the storm—considered the worst ever to hit the northeastern seaboard—left 600 dead, more than 250 of these in Rhode Island. Property damage was estimated at more than $400,000,000, with 60,000 homeless.

During its horrendous rush across the northeastern United States, the hurricane had taken precedence in the nation's newspapers over the impending war in Europe. And when the Munich Agreement was signed on September 30, temporarily relieving a 15-day international crisis, New Englanders can be excused if they felt too busy to give it much attention. They were by that time in the throes of reconstruction. Damaged homes were being repaired or rebuilt, roads and highways cleared, commercial buildings refurbished, and the general business of living was shifting into high gear.

Along the vulnerable coasts of Rhode Island and Connecticut, seaside homes were springing up again and fishing villages were resuming their normal appearance. And throughout the five hard-hit Hamptons on Long Island, the wealthy residents were stubbornly rebuilding their luxurious homes and repairing their prestigious beach and golf clubs.

For these New Englanders were hardy and determined people who found it difficult to believe that such a disaster could ever be repeated. After all, hurricanes *never* struck the northeastern states; gale winds, perhaps, but never hurricanes. Obviously, the terrible catastrophe of 1938 had been the result of a freak storm that had somehow reached farther north than any other—a storm that was meant for Florida but had lost its way. They were sure it would never happen again.

7

Naughty Girl from the Gulf

Cameron, Louisiana (1957)

By the year 1957, the weather bureau had begun its whimsical practice of using female names to identify hurricanes, and this one was called Audrey. Few people paid much attention to Audrey, although she was a girl who needed watching. She was born a little early (few hurricanes have birthdays in June) and perhaps that was one reason people couldn't believe she was much of a woman at all. But those who sampled her strength and vitality—and survived the experience—learned differently.

Audrey's birth was not only premature, it was unimpressive. In fact, even her birth place was questionable. Beginning life on Monday, June 24, she was underweight, an insignificant squall with no foreseeable potential. And she was born in the Gulf of Mexico, some 350 miles southeast of Brownsville, Texas, instead of in the South Atlantic or Caribbean where most self-respecting hurricanes begin.

But on Tuesday, June 25, a Navy pilot in a P2V Neptune,

flying over the then unnamed disturbance, discovered that the winds were circular with an evil eye in the middle, and reported that the storm had suddenly blossomed into a full-fledged hurricane. He also indicated that it was moving sluggishly toward the west coast of Texas and the southwest shoreline of Louisiana. The weather bureau at once christened its first child of the year Audrey.

Alerted to the fact that the Gulf squall now qualified as a true hurricane, the weather bureau promptly sent out warnings. At 10 A.M. on Tuesday a hurricane watch was issued for both the Texas and Louisiana coasts. On Wednesday, June 26, additional warnings included a forecast of high tides and advised all persons residing on the beaches or in low inland areas from the coast to move to higher ground. The warnings were widely disseminated by radio, television and the press. This was 22 hours before the storm actually struck land— plenty of time for people to get the message and move.

Thousands of Texans, in particular, heeded the warnings. Citizens of Galveston—perhaps recalling the dire disaster of 1900—began to leave the city. Some 400 children in four summer camps in the Galveston Bay area were moved inland. At Orange, 2,000 refugees crowded into the three-story courthouse, and all along the coast people fled to points of safety. At Port Arthur, 5,000 coastal homes were evacuated.

As if eager to demonstrate her strength, Audrey took nine lives in the Gulf before she ever reached land. The 78-ton fishing vessel *Keturah* was practically lifted from the water by the winds and hurled against an off-shore oil drilling rig near Galveston Bay, sinking the vessel and sending the nine-man crew to their deaths.

On Thursday morning, June 27, the hurricane roared along the Texas coast, but she was swinging north at the time and gave the Lone Star State only a glancing blow. Some damage was done: Heavy winds tore down power lines and toppled trees; the rain flooded streets; sea water, whipped to a frenzy by the storm, leaped the seawall at Galveston and swamped homes and business buildings; and the top floor of the nine-story Goodhue Hotel in Port Arthur collapsed. But the destruction was slight compared to the total catastrophe that would be visited on the Louisiana coastline the following morning.

Cameron Parish (County) is located in the extreme southwest corner of Louisiana. Its coastal area is mostly marshland, and it harbors such bayou towns as Cameron, Grand Chenier, Creole and Johnsons Bayou. The parish is low, flat, swampy land, with shallow inland lakes scattered about haphazardly. Here and there, on patches of slightly higher ground supporting clusters of old oak trees, lie these tiny towns.

The people are primarily Cajuns, tracing their ancestry back to the Acadians, of French descent, who migrated to Louisiana when they were exiled from Nova Scotia by the British in the last of the eighteenth century. They speak their own peculiar brand of French, sometimes mixed with a little Spanish and English—and when they speak "pure" English it is with a thick French accent. In 1957 there were small enclaves of industry in Cameron Parish, the bulk of it related to off-shore oil drilling. But for the most part, the Cajuns along the parish coastline were shrimp fishermen who made their living in a gamble with the sea.

These were the people who were to feel the cruel impact of Hurricane Audrey. Simple, hardy folk, with something of a stubborn streak, most of them did not take weather bureau warnings seriously. They had been safe in their marshland surroundings for years and found it difficult to believe that anything could upset—much less destroy—their way of life.

Several hundred did move to higher ground, but these were newcomers who had invaded the Cajuns' land when off-shore oil drilling entered the area. The old-timers felt secure in their isolation, and they weren't about to listen to "busybodies" who had nothing more important to do than report the weather. An 80-year-old resident said, "Never in my memory has a tidal wave crossed over this land. I don't expect it will this time." An elderly woman shrugged her shoulders at news that a storm and tidal wave was due to hit Cameron Parish. "I'm not afraid," she said, "because the good Lord has told us he would never destroy this earth by water again." Stubborn and intractable, they were determined to stay in their homes and ride out whatever forces nature threw their way.

It was mid-morning, June 28. Fierce, rain-laden winds, reaching 105 miles an hour, were hammering the flat shoreline of Cameron Parish. Those who had stayed home to face the hurricane were beginning to have second thoughts, but now it was too late to escape. The wind blew savagely; the rain flooded the land. Homes trembled, trees swayed, black clouds brought semi-darkness to the day. Some remembered, belatedly, that a tidal wave had been predicted. How high? How big? Maybe it would never come. The weather bureau could be wrong, you know.

But the tidal wave did arrive, a 20-foot-high tower of water rising out of the sea and heading directly toward Louisiana's defenseless shore. In its way were the towns along the coast, unprotected villages of down-to-earth people who loved this fetid, unsightly marsh so much that they were reluctant to leave it, even in an emergency.

All the bayou towns were flooded by the mighty wave, but Cameron was the hardest hit. Homes either crumbled under the weight of water or were torn from their foundations and carried inland by the wave. The few trees that survived on hillocks were uprooted and sent crashing to the ground. Stores and other business places in the tiny commercial center were shattered and fell in snarled heaps; only two buildings remained standing, the red-brick courthouse and an ice-house made of concrete blocks.

Fishing boats in the harbor were crushed. Some 75-footers were picked up and carried hundreds of yards inland, where they were tossed against buildings. A huge oil drilling barge weighing tons rode the crest of the wave into the town of Cameron, crumpling four fuel storage tanks before coming to a crashing halt on the highway that led north from Cameron to Lake Charles.

Throughout Cameron Parish the bayou dwellers fought for their lives. Some swam, some held tightly to pieces of wood from shattered homes, some clung desperately to trees. Many, who counted themselves lucky, reached small mounds of dry land on the fringe of the flooded area but found that they faced a new danger there. Alligators and poisonous water moccasins thrown up by the waters terrorized them, snapping and striking furiously.

Albert January, along with his wife and three children, managed to climb aboard a floating roof that supported 28 other survivors of the tidal wave's initial assault. But the storm was not finished with them. Another wave swept over the roof and some of the people lost their grip and slid off. Among them were January's wife and children. Undaunted, January leaped into the swirling waters, rounded up his family and got them back on the roof. For hours the survivors clung to their precarious perch. A second wave hit, and again January had to slide into the water and pull his family back to safety. The same thing happened a third time and again January rescued them. But as darkness closed in on the drifting survivors, a fourth wave swept his family into the water, and this time the distressed father could not find them. When daylight came, January and one other man were the only two left on the roof.

Rosemary Quebodeaux was in a home near Cameron with her seven year old niece and six-year-old nephew. As flood waters rose, the trio climbed into the attic. But the raging waters proved too much for the house and it finally caved in.

The children were lost, but Rosemary managed to hang onto a piece of floating debris that carried her across nearby Calcasieu River and deep into the woods. She was saved later by rescue workers.

Shortly before the tidal wave, Theo Thibadeaux rushed his wife, daughter and son to a low hill where they managed to survive as they watched their home break up and sail away on the wave. They lost everything, except what their young daughter had brought with her to the hill—a pale blue parakeet in a cage and a box of bird food.

Norman Wood, a young father, was spared some of his family. Clinging to a large tree for hours as the waters rose around him, he was able to save his wife and two oldest sons, but he lost a third son and his nine-month-old twin babies. Afterward, in a state of shock, he recalled "I held my babies close. But sometimes the body doesn't want to do what the brain tells it to do. I wanted to hold onto my babies, but—" He shook his head and stopped talking.

R. A. Whatley and his wife, Dorothy, were visiting friends when tragedy visited them. In an effort to escape death as the water poured ashore, they climbed into the upper reaches of the house. The house creaked and shook, and when it became obvious that it would break apart, the group quit the building, got into the water, and grabbed onto a tree. Whatley held onto the tree and his wife for eighteen hours before he was rescued. The others died.

One of the great heroes of the storm was Dr. Cecil Clark, the only physician in Cameron. A half hour before the tidal wave struck the town, Dr. Clark left his home for the Cameron Medical Center where he had patients to attend. Although he was aware of the weather predictions for the area, he was sure that his wife, three daughters and a nurse would be safe in their well-constructed home. Two other children were visiting their grandmother in Oak Grove, about twelve miles away.

When the tidal wave smashed ashore the medical center was reduced to ruins, but Dr. Clark was one of those who survived. However, the force and size of the wave had surprised him and he began worrying about his family. He wanted desperately to rush home and determine if they were safe, but at the same time he had an important job to do. Injured and shocked survivors of the great wave were being handed over to him by the dozens for treatment. True to the code of his profession, Dr. Clark stayed at his task, treating the injuries of those who had miraculously escaped death.

When most of the more seriously injured had been treated, Dr. Clark left temporarily to check on the welfare of his family. He waded through knee-deep water to the site of his home, but to his amazement his house had completely disappeared. There was no sign of his wife and children.

Heartsick, he went back to his task of treating more victims of the storm. Sure now that his family was dead, the bereaved, sometimes sobbing physician worked all day and all night, aiding those in need. It was not until the following afternoon, when additional doctors were flown into Cameron, that he agreed to leave his work and make another attempt to find his family. Some time later rescuers discovered Dr. Clark's wife twenty miles from her home, clinging to a large piece of driftwood. Her three daughters and the nurse had been carried away by the flood. The other two children in Oak Grove had been spared.

Throughout Cameron Parish the hurricane created havoc. The towns of Grand Chenier, Creole, Johnsons Bayou and Pecan Island (the latter in Vermillion Parish east of Cameron) also suffered destruction and casualties, although the devastation was not as complete as it was at Cameron. On Pecan Island, loss of human life was light, but 30,000 head of Brahman cattle worth millions of dollars were drowned by the wave.

On the morning of June 29, when Hurricane Audrey finally released its grip on Cameron Parish and moved north, relief forces from the United States government, the American Red Cross, the Coast Guard and other agencies went into action. But accolades should go first to the intrepid men of the Louisiana Forestry Commission who traveled through almost impassable country to reach the hard-hit village of Cameron eighteen hours before any other relief workers arrived.

Desolated Cameron was in dire need of food, water, medical supplies, clothing, generators and other equipment following the storm, and district forester Don McFatter was determined to supply those needs. He contacted the State Police post at Lake Charles, about 40 miles north of Cameron, and offered his services.

"How can you help?" asked state policeman Jerome Hayes.

"I've got trucks, tractors, pickups and twenty-four men," McFatter said.

"Good. But the whole area is a mess and it'll be tough getting through."

"I'd like to try it," said McFatter.

The trucks were loaded and two state policemen assigned to lead the convoy of trucks to Cameron. Sloshing their way over a highway awash with water, the foresters could see nothing but floodwater on either side of them, the remains of the huge tidal wave that had battered the lowlands. Then, just below the town of Hackberry, the convoy came to an abrupt stop. Ahead of them the highway was blocked by an unimaginable mass of wreckage. A huge bulldozer was attempting to push the rubbish to one side.

"How soon can we get through?" McFatter asked the operator of the dozer.

"Hard to say," was the answer. "There's wreckage on the road for two miles."

McFatter decided that perhaps the trucks could be used to help clear the road. He and his men took the ramp boards off their ton-and-a-half truck and tied them crosswise onto the front to form a "blade" that would push the debris ahead of them. But while they were readying the trucks for their new task another hazard entered the picture—poisonous snakes slithered from the water on either side of the road.

"We've got to watch them babies," one man remarked. "You guys keep aworkin'. I've just appointed myself official snake killer."

For a full hour, while the men worked at converting the truck to a bulldozer, the snake killer destroyed poisonous moccasins and rattlers by the dozens.

It was a long, tedious task to clear the two miles of blocked highway. Several hours were spent at this work and when it looked as if the way ahead was clear another problem arose. A mile-long section of the road had been ravaged by deep zigzagging ditches carved into its surface by the hurricane. It took another hour or more for the bulldozer to scoop up dirt from the sides of the road and fill the ditches so that the trucks could pass.

Slowly, with great caution, the trucks rolled over the debris-covered highway. The convoy did not arrive at the Calcasieu River, which it would have to cross to get into Cameron, until after dark.

Fortunately the car ferry used to cross the river had suffered only minor damage and looked ready to take the convoy of trucks across. But another obstacle loomed.

"The ferryboat man was killed in the hurricane," a man told them.

"Isn't there anybody around that knows how to operate it?" McFatter asked.

"Ain't nobody I know of."

McFatter gazed out across the blackish river. Even in the darkness he could see that the river was swollen and turbulent. They would have to find somebody with experience enough to pilot the boat across this last barrier.

It took five hours before they found two men who agreed to

attempt the crossing. They were not experienced ferryboat pilots, but they thought they knew enough about the boat to get it across. McFatter decided there was nothing to do but attempt it.

The plan was to first take the ferryboat out into the main current of the river by itself and, if things worked out right, to return and pick up the trucks. The experimental crossing almost ended in disaster. The two inexperienced men started the motors of the boat and moved out. When the main current caught the ferry the men lost control, and it was swept a quarter of a mile downstream toward the Gulf of Mexico. Fortunately a tugboat was on the river at the time, and it managed to corral the runaway ferry and push it back to the landing. But as it reached the landing area, the ferry crashed into the dock with such force that it heavily damaged both itself and the wharf.

It took another hour of effort to repair the dock and ferryboat so that the trucks could be loaded. Despite the difficulty they experienced on the initial crossing, the two unskilled pilots were certain they could get it across on the second attempt.

The ferryboat inched out into the stream with the heavy load of trucks, carefully avoiding floating debris as it made its cautious way toward the main current. When the ferry came into the current the same thing happened—the rapidly moving downflow caught the boat again and sent it reeling toward the Gulf.

This time, however, the pilots corrected the situation. Gunning the engines, they escaped into smoother waters on the opposite side of the river. They were a half mile downstream by this time and had to make their way back up the river to a landing spot at Cameron.

In the blackness of night the men could not see the awful destruction of the town. But they had heard that the courthouse was still standing and that Civil Defense operations were headquartered there, along with many hapless refugees who had sought shelter in the building during the storm. This was the target toward which the trucks moved.

They had gone only a short distance, however, when the glare of the trucks' headlights illuminated a formidable obstacle. The street was blocked by an oil-drilling rig about 250 feet wide and two stories high. Alongside the rig was a battered shrimp boat. Both had been hurled into the town from the Gulf.

The convoy virtually had to make its own road around these obstacles before heading toward the center of Cameron. Now the foresters noticed the odor of dead animals and humans. Some tied handkerchiefs over their noses to ward off the smell. Their eyes scanned each side of the street as the trucks lumbered on, but they could see no houses standing, only piles of mangled lumber and bricks. In almost the center of town the trucks came to a halt. At least 500 dead cows lay in the street.

Threading its way through the dead animals, the convoy at last pulled up before the courthouse. A harassed state policeman welcomed them heartily. It had taken the convoy twelve hours to make the journey of 40 miles, but they were the first relief agency to reach the stricken city.

The state policeman told McFatter and his men that the only two buildings standing were the courthouse and the icehouse. "There are a lot of those still alive in the courthouse," he said. "We're putting the dead in the icehouse."

For 36 more hours the gritty foresters worked, unloading the supplies they had brought and assisting the victims. By that time other relief groups were moving in—the American Red Cross, Army units, civil defense workers. President Eisenhower had proclaimed Cameron a disaster area and all the facilities of the United States government were thrown into the job of cleaning up debris and taking care of the storm's victims.

Ruined and crumbled buildings form a jagged pattern against the sky following the destructive San Francisco earthquake of 1906.

Courtesy California Historical Society, San Francisco (Bear Photo Service Collection)

The Alaska earthquake of 1964 scissored the ground from beneath Fourth Avenue in Anchorage, sinking buildings to a lower level.

U.S. Army Photograph by B. Bannon Historical and Fine Arts Museum, Anchorage, Alaska

The Galveston hurricane of 1900—most disastrous in American history—tossed railroad cars around like matchsticks in this area of destruction. Ironically, the Deep Water Saloon was unharmed.

Courtesy Rosenberg Library, Galveston. Texas

This was a typical scene in Florida after the 1928 hurricane swept through the Caribbean islands and hit Florida at Palm Beach, killing a total of 4,000 people.

The 1938 hurricane that ravaged the New England states did major damage on Long Island, where homes and posh resorts were leveled. This house and nearby trees were intermingled by the hurricane's fury.

Courtesy United Press International

Hurricane Audrey smashed into Cameron, Louisiana, on June 28, 1957, leaving splintered rubble, wrecked homes, and demolished cars.

Courtesy United Press International

St. Pierre, on Martinique, was reduced to rubble after Mont Pelee, a long-dormant volcano, erupted violently and killed 30,000 people within seconds.

Courtesy United Press International

The Johnstown Flood—fabled in American history—piled an indescribable heap of debris against Stone Bridge. When the debris caught fire, thousands of people who were trapped in the pile-up perished.

Courtesy The Camera Shop, 529 Main Street, Johnstown, Pennsylvania

The flood that roared through Rapid City, South Dakota, in 1972 played macabre tricks on residents. This automobile has been transplanted to the basement of a ruined home.

Courtesy The Rapid City Journal

New York's famous Blizzard of '88 left this wintery scene on New Street in the Battery. The snow lay in huge drifts and ice covered the wires.

Courtesy Museum of the City of New York

Murphysboro, Illinois, was hard hit by the killer tornado that swept through the Midwest in March 1925, devastating 30 towns and claiming the lives of 689 people.

Courtesy Chicago Historical Society

The Palm Sunday tornadoes of 1965 caused widespread damage throughout six midwestern states. A dance hall at Devil's Lake was flattened while nearby buildings survived.

Courtesy D. H. Hurlbut

The sights that relief workers saw in Cameron became imbedded in their minds forever. A fisherman, who had been swept into the Calcasieu River and rescued, wandered around the littered streets sobbing for his father, his pregnant wife and two children who were gone. Two brothers were seen wrapping the bodies of their mother and father in sheets before digging a grave in the marshy soil. A young man comforted his mother as she wept for two daughters lost in the hurricane and told her, "There ain't no use cryin'—we could all be dead." A young boy sat on the courthouse steps, shock reflected on his face. "My brothers are dead," he mumbled. "We don't know where daddy is." A young father, watching workers carry the dead body of his wife out of a swamp, said sadly, "I've got to stay here and try to find my kids. They died with my wife, but I have to find them. I saved four people, but in doing so I lost my family."

Those who by luck or ingenuity managed to remain alive were dazed and shaken. Some stood silently in the shattered streets, gazing in horror at the havoc caused by Audrey. Others wandered aimlessly, their faces expressionless with disbelief, stunned and exhausted people who had survived a nightmare. What they had seen—their friends and kin washed away in blackish floodwater, their homes splintered, everything they had worked for destroyed—would never be erased from their memories.

Within a day or two the floodwaters receded. Those waters carried countless bodies out to sea—and left just as many ashore. For days the bloated forms of humans and cattle littered the entire parish as workers labored to remove them. The official tally of the dead and presumed dead was set at 430, with 40,000 more homeless—both sizable numbers in sparsely settled Cameron Parish. Most of the deaths occurred in the town of Cameron itself. No firm figure ever did emerge on property damage, but oil companies alone placed their losses at $10,000,000.

For days relief workers labored to help those still alive. The sky was dotted with helicopters and the Calcasieu River swarmed with small craft, both picking up refugees and transporting them to Lake Charles, where two hospitals were filled with the injured. Coast Guard cutters plied off-shore areas and deep channels, plucking stranded refugees from floating rooftops and debris. Bulldozers cleared roads so that the Red Cross could bring in medical supplies. Eventually the Red Cross had 80 shelters throughout the parish and was caring for more than 40,000 people.

A heart-rending story came from a 91-year-old woman brought to Lake Charles by helicopter. "In the helicopter," she said, "was a man with a little boy. The little boy was dead, but the man didn't seem to realize it. He kept kissing the boy and talking to him. He kept saying they would be safe soon. It was the saddest thing I've ever seen."

Audrey continued northward, having spent most of her might over the flatlands of Louisiana. Some destruction occurred along her dying path, but nothing comparable to that in Cameron Parish. Audrey's winds spawned tornadoes in Alabama and Mississippi; her rains caused flash floods in Missouri, Indiana and Illinois; western Pennsylvania and New York State were buffeted by gale winds that wrecked power lines and blacked out cities; strong winds were also felt as far north as Maine; and Canada was teased with the last of Audrey's strength.

Sometimes a simple statement can sum up tragedy better than thousands of words. An elderly fisherman caught the horror of Audrey in one short sentence, saying: "It was hell, just hell, from start to finish."

Volcano!

From the beginning of time mankind has been awed and terrorized by erupting volcanoes. In ancient days, men thought that the smoke, lava and rumbling noises issuing from the volcano's crater were triggered by the wrath of the gods. The name volcano, in fact, comes from Volcanus, the Roman god of fire, and an island in the Mediterranean Sea where the god was supposed to dwell was also called Volcano.

Today's volcanologists know considerably more about these pimples on the earth's crust. Simply speaking, a volcano is an opening in the earth's surface beneath which the rock is so hot that it is in a liquid state. This liquified rock is called magma. It rises from chambers as deep as 20 to 40 miles below the surface of the earth.

Magma contains large quantities of gas, composed mainly of superheated steam and, sometimes, noxious elements. The gases are so hot that they exert great pressure, and the magma is forced to escape from its prison. It naturally seeks a weak spot in the earth's crust and breaks through. Thus, a volcano is formed.

Volcanoes are classified in four distinct groups: Hawaiian, Strombolian, Vulcanian and Peleean. Hawaiian volcanoes produce a fluid magma (lava) that usually pours over the rim of the crater with little violence. The Strombolian type has thicker lava from which gases escape with successive explosions. The Vulcanian kind has even heavier lava which can be released only by more violent explosions. And the Peleean volcano is the most violent of all, literally blowing its top and shaking the country for miles around.

Active volcanoes are those that are always "alive" and erupt with great frequency; volcanoes that erupt at regular, predictable intervals are called intermittent; volcanoes that have been quiet for a long time, but not dead enough for scientists to be certain that they will not erupt again, are said to be dormant; and those that have not erupted since the beginning of recorded history are called extinct.

Most volcanoes are located in what is referred to as the Circum-Pacific system. This system fringes the Pacific Ocean, with volcanoes located along the western coast of South America, Central America, Mexico, western United States and Alaska and, on the other side of the Pacific, Japan, the Philippines, the islands of Indonesia and New Zealand. In addition there are active volcanoes in the Atlantic, Caribbean and Indian Oceans.

The most famous—and certainly most romanticized—volcanic eruption occurred in A.D. 79 when Vesuvius destroyed the Roman cities of Pompeii and Herculaneum. Skaptarjökul, in Iceland, erupted in 1783, killing one-fifth of the population; and Krakatoa, between the islands of Java and Sumatra in Indonesia, killed 36,000 people on nearby islands in 1883.

But the cataclysmic eruption of Mont Pelee, on the island of Martinique in the Caribbean, is the only major volcanic tragedy to have occurred in the Western Hemisphere in our time.

8

The Day a City Died
Martinique (1902)

It was on May 8, 1902, that the town of St. Pierre, on the lush West Indies island of Martinique, abruptly died. At exactly 7:50 A.M. on that disastrous morning, 4,583-foot Mont Pelee—a long-dormant volcano—blew its top in one of the world's most cataclysmic explosions.

The French-held island of Martinique shuddered like a stricken giant at the violent eruption. From the yawning mouth of the volcano, a huge black cloud of superheated air and gas emerged that rolled down the sloping side of the mountain like a monstrous tumbleweed. In its path, at the foot of the mountain, lay the harbor town of St. Pierre. Within seconds the cloud swept over the city. Street by street, buildings leaped into instant flame and people were turned into human torches. The hideous black ball—its core later estimated to have been at least 1,500 degrees Fahrenheit—quickly reduced St. Pierre to smoldering ashes. Only two people survived the fiery devastation, and the rest of the populace—more than 30,000—died.

Elapsed time from the moment of eruption to extinction of the city was *less than two minutes!*

The island of Martinique—a French possession since the seventeenth century—is in approximately the center of the Lesser Antilles, a necklace of emerald islands that separates the Caribbean Sea from the Atlantic Ocean. Some forty miles long and twenty miles wide at its bulging center, it is extremely mountainous and covered with green tropical vegetation. Its coastline is punctured by river mouths and placid bays, behind which a chain of mountain peaks forms a jagged pattern against a ceaseless blue sky. At the northern tip of the island, volcanic Mont Pelee rears its lofty head— the undisputed king of all the lesser mountains to the south.

In 1902, St. Pierre, on the western coast of the island and only four miles from Mont Pelee, was Martinique's major city. Twelve miles to the south was Fort-de-France, the capital of the island, but this was a small village that bore no resemblance to glittering St. Pierre. France was proud of St. Pierre; indeed, the French often referred to the city as the "little Paris" or "the Paris of the West" because of its sparkling social life.

Both the city and its people were picturesque. The city stretched for two miles along the coast and, from an approaching ship, it looked like a welcome oasis. The houses, fashioned of stone and stucco, were alive with color. Most of them were painted yellow or bright orange and all had red-tiled roofs. Two main roads ran parallel to the coast, interlaced by cross streets that began at the sea and climbed upward toward the mountain slopes behind the city. With the green mountains as a backdrop, the city had the appeal of a glistening jewel embedded in a costly setting.

In addition to being the social capital of the island, St.

Pierre was also the commercial center. One of its major industries was the rum distillery, and its principal business street, Rue Victor Hugo, was lined with banks, stores and other commercial establishments. The "Paris of the West" was also equipped to cater both to the welfare of the soul and the gratification of the flesh, for it boasted a stately Catholic cathedral and several parish churches, along with a theater where actors from France entertained, cafes, nightclubs and assorted emporiums designed specifically for uninhibited revelry.

The French colonists, whose ancestors had settled on Martinique generations before, represented the elite of the island. They owned and supervised plantations producing tobacco, coffee, cacao and sugarcane. Most of them had built ostentatious villas in the mountains and spent much of their time either relaxing at these summer homes or sipping cognac in St. Pierre's hotels and inns. This wealthy group of Pierrotins—as residents of St. Pierre were called—numbered about 7,000.

Most of the city's 23,000 other inhabitants were blacks. The men—usually bare-chested and dressed in canvas trousers and hats made of bamboo grass—were typically handsome; the women couched their natural beauty in colorful robes and turbans and strode the streets with trays and baskets of salable goods balanced on their heads. The waterfront was a scene of continuous activity as stevedores loaded and unloaded ships calling at what was one of the most profitable ports in the Caribbean.

This was St. Pierre in 1902—a city that had every reason to believe in its future but a city that had no future at all.

Mont Pelee had never been considered much of a threat to those who lived in St. Pierre. Indeed, it was looked upon as a playground. Pierrotins frequently climbed the slope of the mountain and enjoyed picnics near the edge of the main crater. Not only was the high elevation delightfully cool during the hot summer months, but the crater was filled with water for swimming. A second crater, almost a half mile across and lower down the side of the mountain, was completely dry and was called Etang Sec (Dry Pond). Families would descend into this crater for the sheer pleasure of being able to tell others that they had done it.

If anybody remembered that Mont Pelee had erupted in 1851, they were inclined to ignore it. Besides, it had been a feeble eruption. After a few mild rumbles, a shower of fine ash had sifted down on St. Pierre from the crater, and then the volcano had gone back to sleep again. Nobody had any reason to believe that it would wake up.

On the morning of April 25, however, Mont Pelee showed signs of emerging from its long nap. Again there was a mild eruption, and volcanic ash was blown from the main crater and once more fell upon the mountain sides and on the city of St. Pierre. This sudden show of life by their "dead" volcano aroused great curiosity among the townspeople, and families immediately packed picnic baskets and rushed up the slopes to see what was going on. M. Mouttet, French Governor of Martinique, took a slightly more serious view of the matter, however, sending a scientific commission up the mountain to investigate. What both the scientists and the people discovered surprised them: The bone-dry crater of Etang Sec had filled with boiling water and was emitting a strong odor of sulphur.

Still, the people of St. Pierre were not overly concerned. This was merely a repeat of the 1851 eruption, which had amounted to nothing. But on the slopes of the mountain and along the streams and rivers that flowed down the mountainside there were natives who lived in small villages and outlying farms, closer to the strange-acting volcano. These people were more exposed to the whims of Mont Pelee, and some of them left their homes and walked to St. Pierre, feeling that the city offered them better protection.

In St. Pierre the angry mutterings of Mont Pelee served only as a conversation piece. Sophisticated people sat in hotels and bistros discussing the activity of the mountain as casually as they would have appraised a new performance at the theater. After all, St. Pierre was too far away from the volcano—four miles!—to be endangered by even a more violent eruption. And anyway, these amateur volcanologists claimed, the filling of Etang Sec with water was a good sign—it would serve as a safety valve, taking pressure away from the main crater and rendering a serious eruption unlikely.

City officials and the city's newspaper, *Les Colonies,* were also unconcerned. Officials posted no warnings and *Les Colonies* merely mentioned the new activity in passing and assured one and all there was no cause for alarm.

One man who looked upon Mont Pelee's antics with complete dismay was the Very Reverend G. Parel, Vicar-General and Acting Bishop of the Diocese of Martinique. Stationed in Fort-de-France, twelve miles farther from Mont Pelee than St. Pierre, he was observing the volcano's activity closely. On the evening of May 2 he noticed that a change in the nature of Mont Pelee's eruption had occurred—instead of issuing forth grayish ash it was now emitting red-hot cinders. This new turn of events disturbed him and that evening, when he received a telegram from the parish priest of Le Precheur, a small coastal city near St. Pierre, he was convinced something dreadful was about to happen. The telegram read: SERIOUS VOLCANIC ERUPTION. SINCE MORNING WE HAVE BEEN UNDER ASHES. WE ASK YOUR PRAYERS.

This was an alarming report. The Vicar-General went to bed that night wondering what steps he could take to alleviate the priest's concern and finally decided there was nothing a mere human could do to thwart the power of nature.

That night, at a half hour before midnight, the most terrifying detonation yet jarred the citizens of St. Pierre and Fort-de-France from their sleep. Driven from their homes by the awesome explosion, people rushed into the streets and stared up at the brooding mountain. Even in the dark they could see dense black smoke issuing from the crown of Mont Pelee, smoke that was cut through by jagged streaks of lightning. Suddenly a second formidable explosion rocked the entire island, followed by several more. Then the loud detonations stopped and a shower of hot cinders fell on St. Pierre. When daylight came the people of the city looked at their town in amazement. It was no longer the bright colorful city it had been. It was now covered with a ghostly gray ash.

The next morning Vicar-General Parel visited St. Pierre, Le Precheur, Ste. Philoment and Morne Rouge, all coastal cities reasonably close to angry Mont Pelee. He found all of them covered with the same grayish ash, and a strong smell of sulphur permeated the air. The heavy explosions of the night before had induced many more natives living on the slopes of the mountain to flee to the cities on the coast, and each of the towns the Vicar-General visited were now overrun by wild-eyed and fearful people who felt they would be more secure in the towns than in the open. Priests in the churches were busy all day hearing confessions, performing baptismal services, and trying to calm the people who sought solace in the houses of God.

All that day and the following night the volcano exploded at six-hour intervals, and some townsfolk began to entertain the idea of leaving the coastal cities and setting out to sea. But few actually made that move.

Between the period of April 25 and May 2, *Les Colonies* had taken a calm view of Mont Pelee's agitation. Even after the bombardment of May 2, it raised no great alarm. The paper took superficial notice of the increased violence of the volcano and announced optimistically that "the grand excursion to Mont Pelee organized by members of the La Societé Gymnastique et de Tir will take place next Sunday, May 4," adding that if the weather proved favorable "the excursionists will pass a day that they will long keep in pleasant remembrance." On the following day, May 3, the paper reported reluctantly that the excursion had been canceled because the crater had become "absolutely inaccessible."

On May 4 nothing much happened except that the wind changed and blew the gray ash still being lofted by the volcano to the north, where it fell on the cities of Grande Riviere, Basse Point, Macouba and Ajoupa-Bouillon. By May 5 the violence of Mont Pelee seemed to have declined and people in the cities took heart again. Maybe, as they had hoped, the volcano would now quiet down; maybe the worst was over.

But tragedy was building up in the crater known as Etang Sec. Boiling water had now reached its rim, and suddenly the side of the crater collapsed and an avalanche of hot water and mud cascaded down the side of the mountain, joined the Riviere Blanche, and formed a fast-traveling torrent that swept everything before it. As it sped down the mountain the great slide gathered earth until it became a moving mountain of hot mud that rolled over anything and anyone in its path. It raced all the way to the mouth of the Riviere Blanche, where the Guerin sugarworks lay open and unprotected. Workers saw it coming and tried to flee, but the wall of mud rolled over them, killing M. Guerin, the owner, as well as the overseer and twenty-five employees. Nothing remained of the sugarworks except the smokestacks, still standing but bent to one side.

At precisely the same time, in the roadstead of St. Pierre, the sea withdrew, stranding several anchored ships, then rushed back ferociously to flood the streets of the city. This was the first violence to hit the coastal area, and the people acted in curious ways. More refugees from the mountainsides poured into St. Pierre, while others already in the city decided to leave—some by horseback to Fort-de-France and others by ships that were ready to depart for safer ports. The inflow and outflow left the population of St. Pierre about the same—some 30,000 frightened citizens.

May 6 passed in relative quiet, although Mont Pelee continued to rumble deep in the earth. At 4 A.M. on May 7 the volcano again began to roar loudly, this time vomiting black smoke from its main crater. But *Les Colonies* still refused to recognize that St. Pierre could be in any danger. In its issue of May 7, the paper expressed bewilderment at those who were leaving St. Pierre. It said:

> The exodus from St. Pierre is still increasing. From morning to evening and through the whole night one sees only hurrying people carrying packages, trunks, and children, and directing their course elsewhere. The steamers of the Compagnie Girard are no longer empty. We confess that we cannot understand this panic. Where could one be better off than at St. Pierre?

Having thus chided the populace of St. Pierre for its fear, the paper went on to make routine announcements. One report read:

> Thursday being the Feast of the Ascension, the stenographic courses are postponed until next Thursday, May 15. The adult course, which was to have taken place Friday next, is likewise postponed till May 15.

And then the last report from the editor of *Le Colonies* said:

> Our offices being closed tomorrow, our next number will not appear until Friday.

Les Colonies was not the only source of optimistic chatter. Governor Mouttet, anxious to avoid panic in the city of St. Pierre, told the citizenry that a committee formed to investigate the actions of Mont Pelee had reported that nothing justified the evacuation of the city. On May 7, to impress the people with his own confidence, M. Mouttet and his wife left Fort-de-France and moved into St. Pierre, saying, "There is no cause for fear."

But fear persisted. In the roadstead of St. Pierre on May 7, the Italian ship *Orsolina* lay at anchor. Her captain, uneasy about the grumbling volcano, decided to leave. The ship's cargo had only been half loaded and shippers protested his departure, threatening to have port authorities hold up clearance of the ship and put him under arrest. The shippers pointed out, with what they thought to be logic strong enough to convince an Italian skipper, that there was no more danger to St. Pierre from Mont Pelee than there was to Naples from Vesuvius. "If Vesuvius looked like Mont Pelee does right now," the captain retorted, "I'd get out of Naples too!" He sailed, leaving behind a group of frustrated shippers. Seventeen other ships still remained in the harbor.

The fatal day of May 8 was bright and sunny, with hardly a cloud in the sky. It was Ascension Day and the people awoke to the ringing of church bells. Most of the staunchly Catholic populace had risen early to attend eight o'clock mass.

The night had passed with the usual internal growling from Mont Pelee, and the mercurial volcano was now emitting a grayish smoke that rose in a plume from its crater. Still, it was as quiet as it had been for some time, and the people hoped that Ascension Day would be an appropriate time for the Lord to deliver them from the wrath of Mont Pelee.

Stores and shops were closed for the holiday. Only the churches were open, and by 7:30 in the morning they were filled with anxious worshipers thanking the Lord that Mont Pelee's spasmodic eruptions had been no worse and praying that the mountain would now resume its placid ways.

Not everyone was at church. Leon Compere-Leandre, a 28-year-old black shoemaker, sat forlornly on the doorstep in front of his small house on the outskirts of St. Pierre. He was frightened. For several nights he had been awake, listening to the angry thunder from Mont Pelee, and he debated whether to flee the city or to stay and protect his home from whatever was to come.

Looking up now, he noticed the spiral of gray smoke coming from the mountain had turned darker. There seemed more of it, too, for its blackness was beginning to block out the sunshine and cast a dull shadow over the city. He had heard and read that there was no danger, but he wondered if the hopeful editor of *Les Colonies* wasn't being too smug and if Governor Mouttet wasn't playing the fool by moving into the city from Fort-de-France. Like other businessmen, he had closed his shop for the holiday, and he welcomed the opportunity to think things through. . . .

Louis Cyparis was waiting for his breakfast. Meals were the only thing that broke the dull monotony of solitary confinement. Cyparis was a black prisoner being held for murder in a dungeon beneath the ground level of the city of St. Pierre. A small grated window over his cell door was the only opening in his dank cubicle, and on most mornings the grating permitted a feeble ray of light to enter his prison. On this particular morning the sun had seeped through briefly, then faded. Now it was getting darker and Cyparis heard deep rumbling noises. He had been hearing those noises for some time now and assumed that thunderstorms were sweeping over the island. He had been told nothing about Mont Pelee's sudden activity. . . .

Mrs. Thomas T. Prentis, wife of the American counsul in St. Pierre, was up early on the morning of May 8. For two weeks she had been disturbed by the strange convulsions of Mont Pelee, and she was ready to leave St. Pierre the moment her husband thought it necessary. Just a few days before, she had written a letter to her sister in Massachusetts expressing her concern. "We can see Mont Pelee from the rear windows of our house," she wrote, "and although it is nearly four miles away we can hear the roar. The city is covered with ashes. The smell of sulphur is so strong that horses on the street stop and snort, and some of them drop in their harnesses and die from suffocation. Many of the people are obliged to wear handkerchiefs to protect them from the strong fumes of sulphur. My husband assures me that there is no immediate danger, and when there is the least particle of danger we will leave the place. There is an American schooner, *R. F. Morse,* in the harbor, and she will remain here for at least two weeks. If the volcano becomes very bad we shall embark at once and go out to sea."

Mrs. Prentis gazed out of the rear windows of her home and noted the formation of a heavy black cloud over Mont Pelee's cone-shaped top. The cloud was laced with flashes of fire. . . .

At six o'clock on the morning of May 8, the freighter *Roraima* steamed into the harbor of St. Pierre. She was covered with a blanket of gray ash that descended on her as she approached the northern tip of Martinique, but she had proceeded to a point 200 feet offshore where she dropped anchor.

Chief Officer Ellery S. Scott stood at the rail and gazed at Mont Pelee. He noticed that the summit of the volcano was hidden by a wreath of smoke, and when shipping agents came on board he expressed his uneasiness over the appearance of the mountain.

"This is nothing, monsieur," said one of the agents. "You should have been here three days ago when an eruption buried the Guerin factories."

The comment didn't ease Scott's discomfort. He glanced about and noticed the ship's sixteen passengers were on deck looking at the island and its smoke-shrouded mountain. He turned his telescope on the city of St. Pierre. Later he described the scene in these words: "Through the glass I could see people hurrying along the narrow streets to the various churches. Ashes could still be seen on the roofs, but much of the downfall had been swept from the streets so far as I could observe. The people were in their finest attire, and they dressed in gay colors in St. Pierre. It was always interesting to me to see these people in their holiday dress. The headdresses of the women were especially brilliant."

After gazing at the city for some time, Scott turned his telescope toward the summit of Mont Pelee. . . .

M. Fernand Clere, a wealthy planter, was entertaining a large group of relatives and friends at his home in St. Pierre. On the morning of May 8 he was about to sit down to breakfast when he noticed that his barometer was fluttering in a strange manner. Fearing some sort of disaster, M. Clere advised his relatives and friends to leave the city, but they apparently thought their host was over-timid and decided to stay. M. Clere then put his wife and four children into a carriage and set out for his plantation in the mountains, some distance from Mont Pelee. As he passed through St. Pierre he saw Prentis, the American consul, standing with his wife on the balcony of their home.

"I'm leaving the city," M. Clere called out. "You had better come along with me!"

Prentis smiled and shook his head. "There is no danger," he said.

Slowly the horse-drawn carriage wound its way up toward M. Clere's plantation, arriving there just as the black cloud above Mont Pelee's crater grew more ominous. . . .

At 7:50 A.M. the final, ferocious eruption of Mont Pelee took place. At 7:52 A.M. the city of St. Pierre and its 30,000 inhabitants ceased to exist.

It was a deafening explosion, one of the most devastating

volcanic eruptions of all time. The top of Mont Pelee was literally torn apart, and from the innards of the earth a great black ball of heated air and gasses shot into the sky. Within seconds the huge ball had blotted out the sky for fifty miles across. For an instant it clung to the top of the mountain, then rolled down the sloping sides directly toward St. Pierre. It swept over the city and out to sea, burning buildings, ships and people in its path.

There were a few eyewitnesses outside the area covered by the black ball who survived, a handful on land and a dozen or more on ships at sea. From these came the most graphic descriptions—in fact, the only descriptions—of the sudden catastrophe.

An unidentified passenger on the *Roraima* described the destruction of St. Pierre this way:

> I saw St. Pierre destroyed [he related]. It was blotted out by one great flash of fire. Thirty-thousand people were killed at once. Of eighteen vessels lying in the roads, only one, the British ship *Roddam,* escaped and she, I hear, lost more than half on board. It was a dying crew that took her out.
>
> Our boat arrived at St. Pierre early Thursday morning. For hours before we entered the roadstead we could see flames and smoke rising from Mont Pelee. No one on board had any idea of danger. Captain G. T. Muggah was on the bridge and all hands got on deck to see the show. The spectacle was magnificent. As we approached St. Pierre we could distinguish the rolling and leaping of the red flames that belched from the mountain in huge volumes and gushed high in the sky. Enormous clouds of black smoke hung over the volcano.
>
> When we anchored at St. Pierre I noticed the cable steamship *Grappler,* the *Roddam,* three or four other steamers and a number of Italian and Norwegian barks. The flames were then spurting straight up in the air, now and then waving to one side or the other for a moment, and again leaping suddenly higher up. There was a constant muffled roar. It was like the biggest oil refinery in the world burning up on the mountain top.

There was a tremendous explosion soon after we got in. There was no warning. The side of the volcano was ripped out and there hurled straight toward us a solid wall of flame. It sounded like thousands of cannon. . . . Before the volcano burst the landings of St. Pierre were crowded with people. After the explosion not one living being was seen on land.

M. Albert, owner and manager of an estate near St. Pierre, witnessed the eruption from a position on land, and gave a vivid account of his experience:

Mont Pelee had given warning of the destruction that was to come [he said] but we who had looked upon the volcano as harmless did not believe that it would do more than spout fire and steam, as it had done on other occasions. It was a little before eight o'clock on the morning of May 8 that the end came. I was in one of the fields of my estate when the ground trembled under my feet, as if a terrible struggle was going on within the mountain. . . . As I stood still, Mont Pelee seemed to shudder and a moaning sound issued from its crater. It was quite dark, the sun being obscured by ashes and fine volcanic dust. The air was dead about me, so dead that the floating dust seemingly was not disturbed.

Then there was a rending, crashing, grinding noise, which I can only describe as sounding as though every bit of machinery in the world had suddenly broken down. It was deafening, and the flash of light that accompanied it was blinding, more so than any lightning I have every seen. It was like a terrible hurricane, and where a fraction of a second before there had been a perfect calm I felt myself drawn into a vortex and I had to brace myself firmly. It was like a great express train rushing by, and I was drawn by its force.

The mysterious force leveled a row of strong trees, tearing them up by the roots and leaving a bare space of ground fifteen yards wide and more than one hundred yards long. Transfixed, I stood not knowing in what direction to flee. I looked toward Mont Pelee and above its apex formed a great black cloud which reached high into the air. It literally fell upon the city of St. Pierre. It moved with a rapidity that made it impossible for anything to escape it. From the cloud came explosions that sounded as though all the navies of the world were in titantic combat. Lightning played in and out in broad forks, the result being that intense darkness was followed by light that seemed to be magnified in power. That St. Pierre was doomed I knew, but I was prevented from seeing the destruction by a spur of the hill that shut off my view of the city.

When I recovered possession of my senses I ran to my house and collected the members of my family, all of whom were panic-stricken. I hurried them to the seashore where we boarded a small steamship to Fort-de-France. As we drew out to sea in the steamship, Mont Pelee was in the throes of a terrible convulsion. New craters seemed to be opening all about the summit and lava was flowing in broad streams in every direction. My estate was ruined while we were still in sight of it.

One incident suffices to demonstrate the swiftness of St. Pierre's complete destruction. The night shift telegrapher at St. Pierre had just transmitted to the operator in Fort-de-France the latest reports on the volcano. The transmission contained nothing new and mentioned no unusual developments during the night. When he was finished he clicked the key to signal the Fort-de-France operator to reply. The telegrapher in the capital city pressed down his key. The line was dead. No answer came from St. Pierre because the city had died in that split-second.

Leon Compere-Leandre, the shoemaker who was sitting on the doorstep of his home trying to decide whether or not to leave St. Pierre, had his reverie shattered by Mont Pelee's final eruption. The explosion was so violent that it shook the entire island, and Leon felt a shuddering spasm under his feet. He staggered upright and caught a glimpse of the darkening sky and the menacing black ball rolling down the side of the mountain toward the doomed city. Trembling with fear, he turned to enter the house, but a hot wind buffeted him and he felt his body burning as if tongues of flame already were licking at his flesh. With difficulty he made his way into the house and staggered to the table. Three men and a ten-year-old girl were in the tiny house, all of them screaming with pain as the heated air raged over them.

Leon moved to a table and hung over it, wondering if the end was near for him. Then he saw the girl collapse and die in twisting agony, and the three men fled blindly from the room. For what seemed hours—actually about a minute—he held tightly to the table. Then, noticing that the strange hot wind had abated, Leon pushed himself erect and walked into the bedroom where the little girl's father lay. He found the man dead in his bed, already burned to a crisp by the heat. Stumbling into the courtyard he discovered the three men on the ground, their inert bodies charred. The thought crossed his mind, *How can I be alive when the others are all dead?* Screaming, he ran back into the house, threw himself on a bed, and awaited death.

But for some strange reason no one since has been able to explain, death did not come. Instead Leon became aware that the roof of the house was burning and once more he stumbled outside. He saw now that his legs and arms were severely burned and bleeding, but he managed to run six kilometers to the next town—Fonds-Saint-Denis. Once he looked back. All of St. Pierre was in flames. A strangled cry escaped him and he staggered on. Unknown to him, he was one of only two people who had survived the annihilation of St. Pierre.

Louis Cyparis, the prisoner, awaiting a breakfast that would never be served, knew that something more dreadful than a thunderstorm had taken place when Mont Pelee's final paroxysm laid waste to St. Pierre. The noise of the explosion penetrated his underground chamber and the ground beneath his feet vibrated. He rushed to the grate to peer out but staggered back under an onslaught of heated air. The superheated cloud that had engulfed the city had stabbed through the open grating and seered Cyparis' face and body. With a scream of pain he rolled in agony on the dungeon floor.

"Help! Save me!" he yelled, hoping to attract the attention of one of the jailers. But by this time there was no one to hear or to care.

The fiery intrusion in the cell lasted only minutes, then faded. But it left Cyparis in agony, tortured by his burned flesh. For three days he lay groaning in the cell, not knowing what had happened or why no one came to his aid.

On the third day he heard voices over his head and he yelled at the top of his lungs for help. This time he was heard. A rescue party searching the ruins of St. Pierre at once broke open the cell door. When Cyparis was brought out into the light of day, he was amazed to find that the city of St. Pierre no longer existed. In the case of Louis Cyparis, as in the incident involving Leon Compere-Leandre, the blast from the volcano had acted capriciously, leaving him as the only other survivor of the doomed city.

Mrs. Thomas Prentis, wife of the American consul, had suffered misgivings about the peculiar activity of Mont Pelee for weeks. She had studied the threatening mannerisms of the volcano from her rear windows daily, and then had made frequent trips to her front balcony to watch the exodus of people from the city—including their good planter friend, M. Fernand Clere, on the morning of May 8. She yearned secretly to get away from St. Pierre, but her husband had duties to perform there and was sure that Mont Pelee would simmer down in time.

"There's no danger at present," he told her several times. "If real danger threatens, we will leave."

But Prentis and his wife stayed too long. When Mont Pelee exploded on Ascension Day, it took less than two minutes for the fiery air and gasses to snuff out their lives. Two charred bodies were found later in the blackened hulk of their home.

On the freighter *Roraima*, Chief Officer Ellery S. Scott turned his telescope from the city of St. Pierre, where he was watching the colorfully attired people wending their way to and from church, toward the summit of Mont Pelee. At that exact moment the volcano exploded, and Scott witnessed the destruction of St. Pierre in the less than two-minute interval that followed. Afterward he was able to provide a detailed account of the tragedy:

> The whole top of the mountain seemed blown into the air [he related]. The sound that followed was deafening. A great mass of flames, seemingly a mile in diameter, with twisting giant wreaths of smoke, rolled thousands of feet into the air, and then overbalanced and came rolling down the seamed and cracked sides of the mountain. Foothills were overflowed by the onrushing mass. It was not mere flame and smoke. It was molten lava, giant blocks of stone and a hail of smaller stones, with a mass of scalding mud intermingled.
>
> For one brief moment I saw the city of St. Pierre before me. Then it was blotted out by the overwhelming flood. There was no time for the people to flee. They had not even time to pray.

The great black ball of destruction that bounded down the mountain side and swallowed the city of St. Pierre did not stop there. It rolled out into the roadstead where seventeen ships lay at anchor. Scott watched helplessly as the ball billowed out over the water and swept toward his ship. At the last moment, Scott and a few others sought shelter by leaving the open deck and retreating into the innards of the vessel. The move saved Scott's life, but many caught on the deck perished.

When the ball hit, the *Roraima* rolled almost on her port beam-ends, then suddenly went to starboard. The stack, masts and lifeboats were carried away, and dozens of fires broke out. Eventually Scott and other survivors were removed from the burning ship by a rescue craft and taken to a hospital in Fort-de-France.

M. Fernand Clere, the wealthy planter who left St. Pierre just before the catastrophe, was nearing his plantation with his wife and four children when Mont Pelee belched forth its lethal black cloud. M. Clere watched in horror as the cloud tumbled down the mountain slopes toward St. Pierre, but he maintained a remarkable presence of mind under the circumstances. "Knowing how people will exaggerate," he said afterward, "I timed the cloud from the moment it started until it ran into the sea, and found that less than two minutes elapsed."

Watch in hand, M. Clere observed that everything in the path of the rolling cloud burst into flames. He saw his own plantation home leap into flames and saw the great ball of heat roll over his sister's estate in the valley as it aimed its deadly blow at St. Pierre. Two hours later, when he had left his family in a safe place, M. Clere went back to the city of St. Pierre. He found nothing but blackened corpses among the smoldering wreckage of the town. "All were dead," he reported later. "I knew I could do no good there, so I hastened back at the first opportunity and sent my family to Guadeloupe."

In the roadstead of St. Pierre, all but one of the seventeen ships at anchor sank or perished in the flames after the black cloud passed over them. Only the British ship *Roddam*, covered with seething volcanic debris, afire in a dozen places, and with 28 crewmen and most passengers dead, managed to escape. She got away because she happened to have steam up at the time and was ready to sail. Her captain, badly burned, personally took the wheel and guided the ship to the nearby island of St. Lucia. A port official, horrified at the battered condition of the ship and the blackened bodies strewn about the deck, said, "My God, what happened to you?"

"We just came from hell," the captain said.

The full extent of St. Pierre's fate was not known until a relief ship set out from Fort-de-France two days later, when Mont Pelee had once again quieted down and the burned city had cooled enough to permit exploration. Aboard was Vicar-General Parel, along with soldiers, policemen and priests. When the ship rounded an out-jutting of land and moved into the roadsteads of the stricken city, those aboard the ship saw the widespread destruction for the first time. Sixteen ships burned in the harbor, some of them overturned with only blackened hulls above the ash-covered waters. The French cruiser *Suchet* was already on duty, picking up badly injured seamen.

The once-proud city of St. Pierre had disappeared; in its place was smoldering wreckage stretched for two miles along the coast. The Vicar-General turned his glass on the burning city, looking in vain for survivors. He laid the glass down, shaking his head.

"Not a living soul," he said.

Eventually, the Vicar-General and the police, soldiers and priests went ashore. In a letter written to Monseigneur de Cermont, Bishop of Martinique, who was in Paris, the Vicar-General described what he saw:

> We disembark [he wrote] provided with disinfectants, on the Place Bertin, once so full of life and movement. We pick our way through the wreck. The Place is now nothing but a heap of confused ruins. Here and there are decaying bodies, horribly disfigured, and showing by the contraction of the limbs how awful must have been the death agony. Among the seared branches of a fallen tamarind tree, which proved inadequate to protect him, we find the body of a poor creature lying on his back, with his head raised, and his arms stretched to heaven in a

gesture of supplication. The legs are drawn and twisted, the flesh has been torn away from the entrails.

It was only with difficulty that we could reach the cathedral, it being impossible to recognize streets. In the interior of the houses, the walls of which are standing in places, there are still flaming and smoking braziers. Hot stones, iron, lime, cinders, materials of all sorts, scorched the soles of our feet. It was imprudent even to touch the charred walls, which crumbled at the slightest shock.

One of the square cathedral towers, with its four bells, is still upright; but it is riddled throughout, and we dare not approach it. The left tower has been thrown down, together with its great bell. The statue of the Virgin, belonging to the facade, seemed to me to be intact as it lay among the ruins of the cathedral. The walls, with the exception of a part of the apse, have disappeared. We made our way in through the Rue de College and saw several bodies in the ruins. Here, as elsewhere, most of the victims are buried under the piled-up masonry.

Those aboard the Vicar-General's relief ship and others who followed had the unpleasant task of burning or burying 30,000 bodies that quickly putrified in the heat of the sun. They found many of the victims in casual repose, indicating that the black cloud had snuffed out their lives suddenly and painlessly. Others, however, were distorted in agony. Most of the victims caught outside their homes were naked, with their hair burned away and what had been clothing either torn or seared from their bodies; others, indoors, were still covered with their charred clothes. Every stone house in the city had collapsed, and most lay completely in fragments. The entire city was covered by a ghostly white ash that in some places was several feet deep.

Even though the giant ball of volcanic horror had swept the city in less than two minutes, it had enough time to play capricious tricks along the way. In many cases solid objects were pulverized, while fragile articles were left untouched.

Silver stored inside a safe had melted and adhered to the sides of the safe itself. Glass tumblers were fused together by the intense heat, while nearby crockery was not even cracked. In one place a carafe of wine was untouched, but the stems of wine glasses nearby were bent. Although the wall of the military hospital was completely leveled, one section containing the clock still stood. The hands of the timepiece had stopped at 7:52, marking the exact moment that St. Pierre had died.

In all, the volcano's devastation covered an area of about eight square miles. The focal point, of course, was St. Pierre, where there was complete destruction and loss of life. Along either side of the tumbling ball of death was a section where loss of life and damage was reduced. Still farther outside this zone was one where no loss of life occurred, no buildings were damaged, and only vegetation was burned off. On the slopes of the mountain, the rivers that had once flowed with pure water were now either dried up or choked with slowly flowing mud; one mud slide was later estimated to be 80 feet deep.

On May 20, cantankerous Mont Pelee erupted again. This time a violent explosion rent the air over the mountain at 5:15 in the afternoon. The Vicar-General, in Fort-de-France, stood on his balcony and watched the same amazing scene reenacted—a black ball of heated air and gasses again tumbled down the slopes toward St. Pierre. After the eruption, the Vicar-General ordered the *Suchet* to investigate the situation. The report that came back was simply that the remains of St. Pierre had been ravaged again but, since there was little left of the town, the second black ball had failed to increase the damage.

On a recent visit to Martinique we saw a few remaining walls standing in what had been St. Pierre. That was all, for the city that was once called the "Paris of the West" was never rebuilt. Mont Pelee had not only destroyed a city of 30,000 people; it had ended a way of life.

Flood!

And the Lord said, I will destroy man whom I have created from the face of the earth; both man and beast, and the creeping thing, and the fowls of the air; for it repenteth me that I have made them. . . . And behold, I, even I, do bring a flood of waters upon the earth, to destroy all flesh, wherein is the breath of life, from under heaven; and everything that is in the earth shall die. . . . And it came to pass after seven days, that the waters of the flood were upon the earth. . . . And the rain was upon the earth forty days and forty nights.

These sentences from the Book of Genesis describe the biblical world's best-known flood. It is, however, only one of many flood stories that appear in ancient religions, each relating the saga of man's destruction by flood because of his wickedness—and each allowing for one or more survivors to account for man's continuing presence on earth.

Simply stated, a flood results when water overflows its natural or artificial boundaries and spills over onto normally dry land. Such overflows can be either a benefaction or a tragedy to mankind. For example, prior to the construction of the Aswan High Dam on the Nile River, the Egyptians welcomed the annual spring floods because they provided much-needed irrigation to the river's fertile floodplains. On the other hand, the uncontrolled floods of China's Yangtze and Hwang-Ho Rivers have brought repeated disasters, the Hwang-Ho causing 900,000 deaths in 1887 and the Yangtze drowning 100,000 in 1911.

There are four major causes of flood: heavy rainstorms, snowmelt, hurricanes and tsunamis. River floods are usually caused by the first two. In spring, torrential rains can cause a river to rise rapidly and overrun its banks. In winter, a combination of heavy snow and a sudden rise in temperature can create a snowmelt flood that sends rivers over their banks. Coastal floods usually result from the last two causes mentioned. Hurricanes have a double punch, since the winds drive high seas ashore and the clouds empty tons of water to create large areas of inundation. Tsunamis are the result of undersea disturbances, such as earthquakes, that cause huge tidal waves to wash ashore and swamp areas for many miles around.

Floods—particularly those involving rivers—are classified by hydrologists according to magnitude and frequency. A flood of such size that it might conceivably occur only once in 100 years is referred to, logically, as a 100-year flood. This method of predicting the frequency and magnitude of floods is used in engineering flood control projects, such as dams and reservoirs. Most of the time the scientists are accurate in their calculations, but if they err, mankind can become the victim of a great watery terror.

9

America's Most Famous Flood

Johnstown, Pennsylvania (1889)

The Johnstown Flood of 1889 has become one of the most fabled disasters in United States history. It has imbedded itself in the minds of our people, despite the fact that there have been many great catastrophes since. Looming out of the shadows of the past, the Johnstown Flood has piqued the imaginations of three generations and assumed the status of an American legend.

Whether the Johnstown Flood qualifies as a natural disaster or a man-made calamity can be argued. It is true that the earthen dam that burst and flooded Johnstown was crudely built and known to be weakening, and that the dangerous situation had been ignored for years. But it is also true that two months of unprecedented rains were responsible for the extra pressure that caused the dam to crumble. If one wants to be totally accurate, it is safe to say that the inclemency of nature and the mistakes of man combined to produce one of the great disasters in our history.

There were three prominent actors in the great drama that was to unfold on May 31, 1889: a lake named Conemaugh, a dam named South Fork, and a city named Johnstown. Conemaugh Lake was a man-made reservoir high in the mountains of Cambria County, Pennsylvania. It was 3½ miles in length, 1¼ miles in width, and varied in depth from 40 to 100 feet. Nestled among the green-clad mountains, Conemaugh Lake looked serene, beautiful and innocent.

The millions of tons of water in Conemaugh Lake were held within bounds by the South Fork Dam, a huge earthen barricade said to be the largest of its kind in the world. Built in 1862 as a feeder for the Pennsylvania Canal, the dam was 1,000 feet long, 90 feet thick and 120 feet high, and stretched across a deep gorge in the mountain, below which lay such towns as South Fork, Mineral Point, Conemaugh, Woodvale and Johnstown. The dam had served the needs of the canal until the Pennsylvania Railroad pushed through from Philadelphia to Pittsburgh, at which time it was abandoned.

In 1879 a group of wealthy men from Pittsburgh decided that the lake would make a fine location for a private summer resort and purchased both the reservoir and the dam. Among the new owners were such illustrious figures as Andrew Mellon, Henry Frick, Philander Knox and Andrew Carnegie. They immediately built a pretentious clubhouse with adjoining cottages, stocked the lake with bass and pickerel, and christened their new establishment the South Fork Fishing and Hunting Club.

It can be said that this group made a desultory effort to improve the old dam when they purchased it. They plugged a few obvious leaks and built a roadway across the top. But they also impeded drainage by placing a grating over the spillways to prevent their stock of fish from leaving the lake—a mistake that was to prove calamitous.

In the sluice-like gorge 16 miles southeast and 400 feet below the dam was Johnstown, the largest and most prosperous city in the Allegheny Mountain region. It was situated near the foot of the Conemaugh Valley in a pie-shaped wedge formed by the confluence of the Little Conemaugh River and Stony Creek. These two mountain streams merged at a spot called The Point to form the Big Conemaugh, which finally flowed into the Allegheny River above Pittsburgh.

Johnstown began its life in 1800 as a trading center founded by Joseph Johns, a Swiss immigrant. Shortly thereafter, iron, limestone and coal deposits were discovered nearby, and in time these natural resources helped to transform the tiny village into one of the country's top steel-producing cities. Like Pittsburgh, it was smoky and fog-laden most of the time, but the hard-working people—most of them employed by the Cambria Iron Company or the Gautier Wire Works, a subsidiary located in the "suburb" of Conemaugh—drew good wages and were proud of their industrial know-how. Most of the laborers lived in rows of tenements on the flats where the Little Conemaugh and Stony Creek met. White-collar workers lived for the most part on "the heights" that rose abruptly on each side of the city. Johnstown had about 30,000 residents in 1889, and in the gorge between it and the massive dam were the four previously mentioned smaller towns, each with a thousand or two thousand inhabitants.

It cannot be said that the people of Johnstown were unaware that they lived in some danger. Almost every spring there were warnings that the dam might break. But it never had, and the valley people grew tired of hearing about a threatened disaster that never occurred. Besides, Johnstown was far enough away from the dam to assure its people that, even if there were a break, the city would probably be flooded only to a depth of two or three feet.

In any case, citizens of Johnstown were accustomed to minor floods. They had them every spring when rains swelled the Little Conemaugh and Stony Creek, and water rose in the streets of Johnstown to a foot or two. It was a spring ritual for families to battle against rising waters from the rivers, a penalty for living where they did. But it was never dangerous. Children were kept home from school to help their parents move valuable pieces of furniture to upper floors, men sandbagged their houses and places of business, and livestock were driven to higher ground. It was an annual nuisance, something Johnstowners accepted as inevitable.

There was one man, however, who had long been concerned about a possible break in the dam. He was Daniel Morrell, general manager of the Cambria Iron Company. Back in 1879, when he heard that the wealthy new owners of Lake Conemaugh had attempted to repair leaks in the dam, he sent his engineer, John Fulton, to investigate. Fulton came back with the discomforting news that the plugging of leaks had been done in a slipshod manner, that the spillways had been covered with gratings, that discharge pipes were needed to lower the water level if necessary, and that the dam needed a complete overhauling.

When Morrell contacted Benjamin Ruff, the president of the South Fork Fishing and Hunting Club, he was told that the dam was in good shape. "You and your people are in no danger from our enterprise," Ruff said. Later Ruff even rejected an offer from the Cambria Iron Company to assist in strengthening the dam. There was nothing more Morrell could do but drop the matter, but he continued to worry about the dam until his death in 1885.

Now it was Thursday, May 30, 1889—Decoration Day. For two months the weather had been bad. In April there had been a fourteen-inch snowfall that melted rapidly. This was followed by heavy rains that persisted throughout April and May. The Little Conemaugh and Stony Creek were swollen by the torrential downpours, by drainage from the surrounding hills, and by additional water from freshets and tributaries up the valley. Some of the streets of Johnstown were already under water and the citizens accepted stoically the fact that they were in for the usual spring floods.

But this was Decoration Day—a holiday from work—and there were more pleasant things to do than fight the floodwaters. The rain had slackened to a light drizzle, as if in deference to the memorial services. People visited the cemeteries to honor the dead under blackening skies in the morning, then returned to watch the annual parade featuring bands, floats and marching men.

Thick clouds drifted over Johnstown at evening and the drizzle became a driving rain. By nine P.M. a cloudburst began that lasted throughout the night. By early morning on Friday, May 31, the area of the city at The Point, where the two rivers joined, was under two feet of water.

Beset by the seasonal floods, the Cambria Iron Company and the Gautier Wire Works closed down early Friday and the men of the town were home busily moving treasured belongings to upper floors as water crept into their houses. By noon, with the rain still slashing down, the main corner of downtown Johnstown was five feet deep in water and rowboats were being used to transport people about.

In the streets, men talked about the dam, as they had talked every year for decades.

"You think the dam will hold?"

"She always does, don't she?"

"You don't think there's danger?"

"Naw. All I know is I been listenin' to warnin's about the dam for years and nothin's ever happened. I reckon it'll continue to hold for as long as any of us are alive."

Meanwhile, at the dam itself, a civil engineer named John Parke watched with alarm as the level of Lake Conemaugh rose almost three inches in twenty minutes of torrential rain. Already the water was within six inches of the embankment's crest and Parke decided that something had to be done to relieve pressure on the dam. With a crew of workmen who were on hand to do plumbing work at the clubhouse, he descended to the bottom of the dam. He noticed at once that the spillways, which had been covered with gratings, were clogged with debris. Parke and his men worked feverishly trying to remove the gratings but they would not budge.

Parke glanced up apprehensively at the earthen rampart towering over him. Already water spurted from leaks in the face of the dam.

"Maybe we can cut a new spillway through," Parke suggested, even though he knew it was a forlorn hope.

The men frantically tried to cut another spillway, but they could make no progress against the heavy clay soil.

At noon the waters of Lake Conemaugh began to roll over the crest of the dam, pouring down in a steady cascade. Parke knew it was the beginning of the end. On horseback, he raced into the nearest town to the dam—South Fork, four miles away. He informed the telegrapher there to warn all cities in the valley that the dam was about to burst.

At this point there is some dispute as to what happened. One story is that Johnstown and other villages in the path of the coming flood received no warning because the heavy rainstorms had already downed wires in the area. Another source has it that messages about the impending disaster did reach Johnstown over telegraph wires owned by the B & O Railroad. Three messages, it is claimed, got through:

1 P.M.—The dam is in bad shape.
1:52 P.M.—The water is running over the breast of the dam in the center and the west side is becoming dangerous.
2:25 P.M.—The dam is getting worse and may possibly go.

Whatever messages may or may not have been received in Johnstown, few people left the city. A handful—considered timid by their neighbors—climbed into the hills, mainly to get away from already flooded homes. But most people stayed. They could not imagine a catastrophe of the magnitude that was about to descend on them.

At 3 P.M. the top of the embankment began to crumble from the waters pouring over it. Minutes later the waters had cut a "V" in the top of the dam. At 3:15 P.M. the end came. The entire center of the dam exploded outward—or as one eyewitness described it "the whole dam just moved forward"—and into the 400-foot opening the waters of Lake Conemaugh poured forth like a giant Niagara.

It was later estimated that, in its initial burst through the shattered dam, twenty million tons of water swept ninety thousand cubic yards of earth and stone toward the vulnerable towns that lay before it. The avalanche of water and mud quickly reached a height of 50 feet as it roared through the narrow valley. On its way it collected trees, houses, boulders, logs and other debris, and this heavy mass of rubble was to do more damage to the towns in its path than the raging water itself.

South Fork, four miles from the dam, was the first victim. Four-fifths of the town was swept away in seconds. Some of the townspeople had fled to higher ground, and they watched in amazement as the torrent uprooted giant trees, leveled barns, and lifted houses off their foundations and hurled them downstream.

Just before the dam broke, George Lamb, a South Fork farmer, moved his family to high ground. Thinking he still had time, he decided to return to his farm to retrieve his prize pig. He had descended only half way to his home when he heard a mighty roar from the dam and looked up to see a wall of water bearing down on him. Lamb scrambled 100 feet up the mountain in 50 seconds to escape the giant wave. Then he turned to see his farmhouse torn from its foundation, whirled around like a toy, and swallowed up in the rush of the muddy waters.

In the South Fork railroad station the crack New York-

Chicago Limited stood on a siding. There had been a landslide ahead, and the train, carrying 56 passengers, was waiting for track crews to clear the way. The engineer caught a glimpse of the wall of water and debris sweeping down on the town of South Fork and took quick action. At the greatest speed possible from a standing start, he raced the train across an 80-foot bridge spanning the Little Conemaugh and up the tracks on the other side of the gorge to a point of safety. There he stopped the train and watched with horror as the debris-laden avalanche smashed into the bridge, tossed it in the air, and carried it down the valley.

The tiny village of Mineral Point, four miles from South Fork, was next in the path of the floodwaters. It was completely erased from the map. Eight hundred of its 1,000 people died within seconds. Houses, a woodworking plant and a few stores on the main street were added to the mountain of odds-and-ends pushed forward by the water.

The avalanche was now traveling at about 40 miles an hour, but occasionally it would stop almost completely as debris obstructed its path. But the weight of water would win out, and the battering-ram of debris would again pick up speed and move down the valley gorge.

Conemaugh, a town of 2,500 six miles from Mineral Point, was next to feel the brunt of the flood. Here, in the Pennsylvania Railroad yards, seven cars and the engine of the Day Express sat waiting. The train had been on a siding for three hours, waiting for the normal floodwaters of spring to clear the tracks ahead of it. The passengers were nervous. From the security of the cars they had been observing the heavy rains and wondering about the reliability of the dam behind them. When word reached the conductor that the dam might break, he rushed aboard and ordered the passengers to leave the train and climb to higher ground. Only eleven of them made it before the rushing waters struck; 26 were drowned.

What the flood did to the railroad yard was unbelievable. It swept the Day Express before it, carrying all seven cars and the engine downstream. To this prize it added a 16-stall roundhouse, 315 freight cars, 33 locomotives weighing 75 tons each, and 18 passenger cars. It also uprooted the Gautier Wire Works, taking with it 200 reels of steel cable and barbed wire weighing 200,000 pounds. All of this, along with more houses, trees and other debris, rushed downstream toward the flood's ultimate target—Johnstown.

There were several people aboard the Day Express who experienced hair-raising adventures. Among those still in the passenger coach of the train when the flood hit was Charles Richwood and his bride of one day, Edith. The water struck the train with thunderous force, moving it off the tracks and carrying it forward. A window was open near Richwood and his bride, and the young man shoved his wife through into the surging waters. Following her, he fought his way to the surface, and miraculously managed to climb on top of the railroad car in which they had been sitting moments before.

Seconds later the car crashed against debris carried by the flood and the honeymooners were thrown free. Swimming desperately, they reached and climbed aboard the floating roof of a building on which twenty other persons sat. This haven lasted only a few minutes. Directly ahead of the floating roof was the Gautier Wire Works, which the flood had not yet reached. Tons of molten metal in cupolas lay directly in their path and Richwood realized that if the roof struck the Wire Works they would be burned to death.

Clinging to each other, the two intrepid young people left their raft and swam toward a group of men standing on an elevated section of shoreline out of reach of the floodwaters. They were saved when a courageous young man leaped into the waters and hauled them to safety.

John Barr, a conductor in charge of one of the Pullman cars, saw the wall of water descending on the train and later described it as "a mountain moving toward me." He shouted to all passengers to run to higher ground. Then he noticed that John Davis, who was traveling with his invalid wife and two children, ages four and six, was struggling to get his wife off the car. Barr went to help him but Davis waved him off.

"Take the two children and run up into the hills," he said.

Barr grabbed the youngsters, one under each arm, and raced up the hill with the water right at his heels. He ran 200 yards before he was out of danger. Depositing the two children on solid ground, he looked back at the train he had left. The mighty flood caught it and swept it away. John Davis and his wife were never seen again.

A woman known only as Miss Maloney was a passenger on the same train. She was in the parlor car when the conductor advised all passengers to take to the hills. She started to leave, then suddenly decided that remaining in the car would be safer than exposing herself to the savagery of floodwaters. Realizing she might not survive in any case, she ripped a piece of material from her skirt, wrote her name on it in indelible ink, and tied it securely around her waist. Minutes later the wall of debris-carrying water struck the parlor car, drove it from its tracks, but in this case did not take it down the river. When the flood receded the conductor went back to the car, fully expecting to find Miss Maloney dead. Instead he found that Miss Maloney had managed to stay afloat in the tumbling car, which had not been completely flooded.

The flood roared on. One mile farther downstream was Woodvale, a suburb on the edge of Johnstown. It was systematically demolished and more than 300 people perished in a matter of seconds. A tannery, a woolen mill, a streetcar shed with 68 horses, and more homes were added to the rubble carried by the flood.

Johnstown was now just one mile and a few minutes away from disaster. . . .

Reverend David J. Beale, pastor of the Presbyterian Church in Johnstown, was busy at home, working on his sermon. He, his wife, and his two sons, twelve and fourteen, had just completed the task of moving their furniture to the second floor to protect it from the annual floodwaters lapping at the front door. Now the Reverend was engrossed, his pen gliding quickly over the pages of the sermon with which he hoped to inspire his congregation at Sunday services.

Shortly after 4 P.M., he heard a rushing sound that he immediately took to be floodwaters approaching. Frightened, he grabbed the Bible from his desk and raced into the parlor. His family was there, along with three parishioners who had taken shelter with them. He ordered them all to the second floor.

They moved none too soon. The waters invaded the second floor right behind the fleeing pastor and his charges and kept right on going until they reached the attic. Even in the attic the water was already swishing around their ankles.

The minister fell to his knees and led his family and visitors in prayer. Then he read the verses of the 46th Psalm:

"God is our refuge and strength, a very present help in trouble. Therefore will not we fear, though the earth be removed and though the mountains be carried into the midst of the sea."

For a long time the group knelt there in the water, their heads bowed. . . .

Gertrude Quinn, eight-years-old, her three sisters, Marie, Helen, and Rosemary, and a brother Vincent were being cared for in their mother's absence by their Aunt Abbie and a nurse named Libby. On the morning of the flood their father, James Quinn, was busy sandbagging a dry goods store he owned in the business section of town, and Vincent was helping an uncle move merchandise from his clothing store to a safer place.

The spring waters were a foot deep around the children's home at Main and Jackson streets, and young Gertrude took off her shoes and socks and waded around in it. When her father returned he ordered her inside. He expressed fears about the South Fork Dam and told everyone to be alert for a rush to the hills in an emergency. Aunt Abbie thought he was super-cautious, however, and pointed out to him that their big brick house was sturdy and would never succumb to a flood, however serious.

But Gertrude knew her father was nervous and she watched him pace the floor and look anxiously out the windows from time to time. Then, shortly after 4 P.M., he heard the sound he had dreaded—a roaring noise in the distance that meant only one thing to him. Water was rushing toward them. The dam had collapsed!

Without a moment's hesitation Quinn picked up his youngest daughter, Marie, who was ill, and headed for higher ground, with Rosemary and Helen right behind him. He shouted to Gertrude, Aunt Abbie and the nurse to follow him. When he reached safe ground he turned around to find that neither Gertrude nor the two women had left the house. Impatient with what he knew must be Aunt Abbie's reluctance to leave, he started back down to get them—just in time to see his house swept away by the giant wave. . . .

Dr. W. W. Walters, like everyone else in Johnstown, had taken the elementary precaution of moving furniture and other possessions to the second floor of his home near the center of town. He, his wife, and two daughters were apprehensive about the spring flood because it seemed more severe than in other years. But they had no real fear of the dam giving way until they, too, were alerted by the thundering sound of an approaching cataract. Immediately they fled to the second floor of the house, and Dr. Walters stood at the head of the stairs looking down as his living room filled with water. Suddenly his front door burst open and, to his amazement, Dr. Walters saw a railroad car passing by his house where there were no tracks.

As the water rose to threaten the second floor, the Walters took refuge in the attic. When it lapped at the attic floor, the doctor chopped a hole in the ceiling with an axe and the family climbed out onto the perilously slanted roof. Dr. Walters brought a long piece of stout rope he had found in the attic and with it he bound all members of the family together and then tied them securely to the chimney. As long as the roof held together, he thought, they would be able to ride out the storm. . . .

Johnstown was not hit by a flood. It was smashed to pieces by a battering-ram. For sixteen miles, down the Conemaugh Valley, the raging water had accumulated its mountain of debris, and the giant wave was still fifty feet high and moving tens of thousands of tons of wreckage at a speed of sixty miles an hour when it bore down on Johnstown. It contained thousands of trees; hundreds of houses from the villages of South Fork, Mineral Point, Conemaugh and Woodvale; more hundreds of human beings, some alive, some dead; horses, dogs, cats and even rats; more than 100 miles of telegraph wires still strung to poles; a tangled mass of barbed wire and cable from the Gautier Wire Works; 50 miles of railroad track, along with ties, spurs, and entire switch towers; 33 locomotives weighing 75 tons each; more than 300 freight cars and 18 passenger cars; the battered remains of the Conemaugh roundhouse; and a mishmash of debris that included motors, machinery, boilers, pig iron, brick, stone, lumber.

All this, traveling a mile a minute, bulldozed its way into Johnstown. Block by block the city was leveled. People who had taken refuge in their attics or on the roofs of their houses were swept up in the maelstrom of destruction. Some were crushed in the debris, others carried along with it. A few, halfway up the mountainside and on the edge of disaster, were spared. A handful caught in the avalanche were saved by some freakish accident. But most were gathered up in the lethal cascade. The strongest building in town, the Hulbert Hotel, where 51 people had taken refuge, was reduced to rubble by the torrent.

But suddenly this monstrous juggernaut of water and

wreckage was stopped in its tracks. Just below The Point was a solidly built bridge. Stone Bridge, as it was called, carried the Pennsylvania Railroad tracks over the Conemaugh River. It was a four-track structure, fifty feet wide on the top, thirty-two in height, and consisted of seven sixty-foot stone arches. It crossed the river diagonally, which no doubt saved it from instant destruction, since the onslaught hit the bridge only a glancing blow. But the fact that the bridge did not collapse actually spawned an additional tragedy.

When the floodwaters struck the bridge, the mountain of debris came to a crashing halt. Entire houses were thrown over the bridge like volleyballs over a net, but most of the tangled wreckage piled up. The 60-foot archways quickly became plugged with trees, boulders, brick and other rubble. The driving force of the floodwaters piled lumber, railroad cars, parts of factories, and houses against the unyielding bridge, to create a new dam 70 feet high. In this hideous pile-up hundreds of people were trapped. Some were still in their homes. Others clung to rooftops. Many were simply pinned in the pile of rubble, held fast by a leg or arm. Many were already dead, mangled beyond recognition by the shifting debris; others were grievously injured but remained alive.

The floodwaters, momentarily diverted by the jam-up at the bridge, surged backward. People who had by some miracle escaped death as the thundering current raced past them were now caught in the backwash. One eyewitness, describing the backward rush of water, said, "The flood struck first against the jam, and thus lost most of its fierce energy, flowing thence (backward) in a heavy stream which tossed about houses in a most fantastic way so that part of the town looked like a child's toy village poured out of a box haphazardly. About half of the loss of life was in this district, for all Johnstown became speedily a lake twenty or more feet deep."

Reverend Beale, in the attic of his home with his family

and three parishioners, gazed out the window at the havoc being wrought by the giant flood. He watched as the great hill of debris piled up against Stone Bridge. He saw houses and rooftops float by his window and he wondered why his own house had not been moved from its foundation and decided that it must be the will of the Lord.

Suddenly a man floating in the water crashed through the window and sprawled on the attic floor. Amazed, Reverend Beale bent over him.

"Where did you come from?" he asked.

"Woodvale," the man gasped.

The minister returned to the window. He saw more people riding roofs past his house. He saw the backwash, then watched the flood surge forward again. This time the water got past the bridge, some of it going over the top and some seeping through holes gouged in the rubble. His own home trembled violently and he realized that it would not hold up much longer. He saw only one way out. If he could get his family to make their way over the top of the debris at the bridge, they could reach Alma Hall, a stout building that still stood, most of it above the water level, on higher ground beyond the bridge.

It was a treacherous journey, but the Reverend and his flock made it. As he described it later, they reached Alma Hall by "walking and jumping from one house or roof or boxcar to another, sometimes compelled to bridge over deep, watery spaces with loose boards or planks."

When James Quinn saw his house swept away by the flood, he was convinced that his daughter Gertrude, Aunt Abbie and nurse Libby were lost. But, as the brick house crumbled, something akin to a miracle saved young Gertrude.

The young girl and two women had taken refuge on the third floor of the house, and when the sledge hammer of debris rammed against it the house shuddered and plaster fell from the ceiling. Aunt Abbie, who had been so certain that the house would hold up, now was just as certain that it wouldn't. She ordered Gertrude and the nurse to fall to their knees and pray, saying, "This is the end of the world and we're all going to die together."

Suddenly the walls cracked and floodwaters entered the house. Gertrude leaped up and went to the window. A muddy mass of lumber, refuse and other trash was passing the house, and Gertrude jumped from the window and landed squarely on a mud-soaked mattress just as the house crumbled and Aunt Abbie and the nurse went to their deaths.

Gertrude screamed for help but there was no one around to aid her. Once she saw a man float by on a roof but he paid no attention to her plea. She cried out again as she passed a building with people perched on the roof. Maxwell McAchren, a burly mill worker, took sympathy on the young girl, leaped into the water and swam toward her with powerful strokes. When he reached the muddy mattress on which Gertrude sat, he climbed on and tried to comfort her, saying, "We'll get out of this somehow, Miss, that we will."

They did, too. Downstream two men with long poles stood on a hillside just above the flood's crest pulling people from the swollen waters. They managed to get both Gertrude and McAchren onto the hillside.

When Quinn later found that Gertrude had been saved, his joy was tempered with sadness. His son, Vincent, who had been helping his uncle at the clothing store, perished.

Dr. W. W. Walters and his family, who had tied themselves to the chimney of their home, prayed that their house would withstand the pressures of the flood and that they would remain safely on the roof until the waters subsided. As they clustered around the chimney two horrifying events took place before their eyes. The brick house of Benjamin Hoffman, their next door neighbor, suddenly collapsed and twelve members of the Hoffman family were killed. Then Dr. Hezekiah W. Marbourg, an associate of Dr. Walters, came floating by on the roof of his house. While Dr. Walters and his family watched helplessly, a freight car crashed against the roof and knocked Dr. Marbourg into the swirling waters.

The same freight car, as if on a mission of vengeance, then aimed its weight at Dr. Walters' home. There was a tremendous impact and the house was ripped from its foundation. It floated down the street for about 150 feet and became trapped in a mass of wreckage. When Dr. Walters was convinced that the house was wedged securely in the debris, he ordered his family back into the attic. There they stayed for two nights, without food or water, before the flood receded enough for them to climb down and walk across the tangled bed of wreckage to firm ground.

Many freakish things happened as the debris-loaded floodwaters raged through Johnstown. A boy safely perched on high ground saw the Eureka Skating Rink floating in the waters "like a liner going down New York harbor." Clinging to the slanted roof were scores of refugees. All of them drowned when the rink suddenly sank beneath the huge wave that carried it. One man put his wife and three children in the Hulbert Hotel because it was the firmest building in town, then returned to his jerry-built home to shore it up against the flooding of Stony Creek. When the dam collapsed the Hulbert House was destroyed and the man's family was killed; he survived in his rickety house. Twelve-year-old John Thomas was sitting with his legs dangling from a second story window of his father's department store when two buildings across the street were lifted from their foundations and carried along on the crest of the flood. Hardly had the lad recovered from his surprise when a locomotive crashed into the front of the store next door and plunged into the basement. Abe Smithers, a lawyer, was eating a late lunch at home when the flood hit, broke up his house, and dumped him into the waters. He was carried a quarter-of-a-mile downstream and hurled through the window of a flooded building into *his own law office!* One man straddled a telephone pole and rode it like a horse down most of the Conemaugh Valley before he was rescued. And a five-month-old baby, lying on the floor of a house, rode the floodwaters for 75 miles all the way to Pittsburgh, where rescuers took him off, uninjured.

But what happened at Stone Bridge, where an indescribable mass of debris continued to pile up, topped everything else that befell luckless Johnstown. Within minutes of the crash of debris against the bridge, the wreckage of every building in a thickly-settled district of town three miles long and half a mile wide—along with an unbelievable accumulation of other rubble picked up in the flood's sixteen-mile journey through the Conemaugh Valley—was stacked mountain-high for thirty city blocks. Trapped in this ghastly pile-up were an estimated 2,000 people, at least half of them still alive but unable to extricate themselves.

Then the great mass caught fire.

In retrospect, the fire at Stone Bridge was predictable. Many homes in the jigsaw puzzle of debris had coal stoves burning when they were swept against the pile-up, and these stoves spilled their red-hot contents over the heap of rubble. In addition, leakage from several wrecked railroad cars carrying crude petroleum spread over the pile-up. These two factors combined to cause a holocaust.

It started at 5:45 P.M., and within a few minutes the Stone Bridge area became an inferno. Besides the 2,000 people half buried in the wreckage, there were also dozens of rescue workers swarming over the pile-up trying desperately to free the living victims. When the fire started, these rescuers bravely stayed upon the burning wreckage, working to free people before the flames reached them. Men, women and children, pinned in the tangled rubble, prayed and cried for help as the flames crept closer. Eventually the fire reached out for them, and amidst cries of agony they died.

Some lucky ones managed to free themselves and escape. Rose Clark, 19, tried frantically to avoid the fire, but her foot was caught in the frozen grip of a man who had died. A rescuer finally hacked off the dead man's arm and set the girl free. Another man, held fast in the debris, actually cut off his own arm to get away. Several victims perished because they were entangled hopelessly in wire from the Gautier Wire Works.

Nightfall added to the chaos. Those viewing the flood and fire from higher ground watched the flames dance over the jam-up like red demons in the darkness and listened helplessly to the screams of the dying. One of the witnesses was an editor of the *Daily Tribune,* who later described the scene this way: "The houses, mountain-high, took fire and burned with all the fury of the hell you read about—cremation alive in your own home, perhaps a mile from its foundations; dear ones slowly consumed before your eyes, and the same fate your own a moment later."

By dawn on the morning of June 1 the sullen gray clouds that had covered the area for a week had disappeared and patches of blue widened overhead. It was obviously going to be a beautiful day, but the ugliness left by the great flood scarred nature's new mood. To the people who had spent the night on the hillsides the light of morning revealed a panorama of unimaginable destruction. Wet, cold and hungry, the people stared down at disaster and, even in their own misery, thanked God for having been spared.

The water had receded from the night before, much of it having seeped through the great jam at Stone Bridge to wreak further devastation on towns below Johnstown—

Cambria City, Sang Hollow, Morrellville. But Johnstown had been the focal point of the flood. A large portion of the town was stacked up at Stone Bridge in a mountain of fiercely burning rubble that would continue to burn for two days more. The fire that had raged all night had not noticeably reduced the size of the 50-foot mass of debris, and behind the great pile-up were other imposing mounds of wreckage. Overturned houses, railroad cars, locomotives, bricks and human and animal corpses were strewn about in the mud as if by the hand of a careless giant.

All night long the sleepless people on the hillsides had listened to the pitiful wailing as the victims trapped in the bridge pile-up burned to death. Now there was silence. By this time people either had escaped the fire or had been cremated by it. The quietude that often follows disaster had settled like a pall over what was left of the city.

What was left? Two churches, the B & O Railroad Station, Alma Hall, a few scattered homes. Except for these few structures, Johnstown had disappeared.

For those who remained alive in Johnstown the problem of reconstruction was almost insurmountable. Cleaning up the rubble of the city would take weeks, possibly months. Rebuilding would take years. Recovering from the horrible deaths of fathers, mothers and children would take a lifetime. That morning the people came down from the hills to look for their loved ones. Wading through knee-deep water, sloshing through sticky mud, they explored the wreckage of their homes and uncovered the bodies of people who had once been dear to them.

Many victims of the flood were never found. A great number had been carried away by the waters or turned into charred, unrecognizable corpses. Morgues were set up in the remains of the few buildings still standing, and hundreds of unidentified corpses were given numbers. The sun rose quickly that morning, casting down its warm rays and increasing the possibility of an epidemic. The big fire at the bridge burned incessantly, and there was no way to defend against it or put it out. There was no medicine, no food. Nor was there gas or electricity. Telegraph and telephone lines were down, and there was no communication with other cities.

But word of Johnstown's tragedy did get out. Pittsburgh was the first major city to hear of it, and from there the news spread across the nation. Within 24 hours, relief trains were headed for the stricken area, carrying food, medicine, lumber, blankets, coffins, embalming fluid, and undertakers.

The great pile-up at Stone Bridge presented a problem for the 6,000 relief workers—some from Johnstown and others sent from Pittsburgh and New York—and it was not until a professional dynamiter arrived at the scene that progress in reducing the mass of rubble was made. For almost a week the Conemaugh Valley echoed with explosions that eventually tore apart the entangled debris.

Many men and women did commendable work in the aftermath of Johnstown's tragedy, but none surpassed the efforts of a tiny 67-year-old spinster named Clara Barton. She arrived with 50 members of a newly-organized group called the American Red Cross. Johnstown was the first major test for Clara Barton and her companions, and they made the most of it. Clara Barton worked with little sleep, directing her small band of relief workers and others who offered help in distributing food, clothing, blankets, medicine and other needed supplies. She set up a crude hospital for the injured, and erected tents and jerry-built shacks for survivors. She stayed five months, and did a job that not only brought relief to sorely-pressed Johnstown but established the American Red Cross as the country's foremost relief agency.

Out of great tragedies arise many myths. One of the most fetching stories to come out of the Johnstown Flood was that of Daniel Peyton, the so-called "Paul Revere of the Conemaugh." Peyton was credited with riding a great white horse from South Fork to Johnstown ahead of the great wall of water sweeping down the Conemaugh Valley. Despite the fact that there was no Daniel Peyton, and that such a ride ahead of the fast-moving waters would have been physically impossible, this legend was presented as truth for many years.

The truth, without the embroidery of myths, was sufficiently dramatic. A total of 2,200 people lost their lives in the great flood, 300 of these in the funeral pyre at Stone Bridge. Ninety-nine families consisting of two to ten persons were completely wiped out. Nearly 100 children lost both parents and some 200 lost a father or a mother. Property damage was estimated at more than $18,000,000—an immense sum in those days.

There was no need to rebuild the South Fork Dam, because Conemaugh Lake had drained itself dry within an hour after the dam burst. But Johnstown continued to have its annual spring overflows in following years as rains swelled the Little Conemaugh and Stony Creek, and in 1936 a flood that took 25 lives occurred. President Franklin Delano Roosevelt visited Johnstown in August of that year and promised federal help. By 1943 a flood control project consisting of nine miles of concrete channel was completed. Today Johnstown calls itself the Flood-Free City.

It may be. But in Johnstown's Grandview Cemetery there are 800 unmarked graves of flood victims who were never identified—a grim reminder of one of America's most dreadful disasters.

10

The Black Hills' Rain of Terror
Rapid City, South Dakota (1972)

It was June 2, 1972 and the tourist season in South Dakota's Black Hills had already begun. Hundreds of people were at Mount Rushmore, gazing at the granite faces of George Washington, Thomas Jefferson, Abraham Lincoln and Theodore Roosevelt. Vacationers roamed through Custer State Park with poised cameras, hoping to capture on film one of the largest bison herds in the world. Campers in tents and trailers were scattered throughout the picturesque mountains, and motorists snaked their way along Needles Highway, marveling at the granite spires that give the road its name. At Sylvan Lake, a pristine pool surrounded by mammoth rock formations, fishermen angled for bass and pike, while boaters enjoyed precious moments of relaxation gliding through the serene waters. Many tourists stared in awe at the partially-completed Crazy Horse Memorial, carved in the side of a cliff, or explored the meandering pathways of Wind Cave. And those with a sense of history experienced a closeness with the Old West by walking through the frontier streets of Deadwood and visiting the graves of Wild Bill Hickok and Calamity Jane on nearby Boot Hill.

In Rapid City—a town of 43,000 that served as the eastern gateway to the Black Hills—families explored Dinosaur Park, where life-size reproductions of prehistoric animals towered above them. The local dog track was operating and, in the evening, a 70-piece band from Wadgassen, West Germany, was scheduled to play before a packed house at the Stevens High School auditorium.

Other things were happening, too. In an area that was about to receive a torrential downpour, the South Dakota School of Mines had two airplanes in the air seeding the clouds—not because rain was needed but purely as a scientific experiment. (The scientists later claimed that their cloud-seeding had nothing to do with what followed, clearing themselves of responsibility by admitting their own failure.) A convention of 500 doctors, lawyers, and clergymen were in town for a seminar entitled *Death and the Dying Patient*. And a repertory theater group was rehearsing the play *You Know I Can't Hear You When the Water's Running*.

Then the rains came.

It was late afternoon when a light shower began to fall in the Black Hills west of Rapid City. The rain was not unexpected; the weather forecast that day was for "scattered showers and thunderstorms." Campers holed up in their tents and trailers, and tourists took shelter in motels or their cars, content to wait until the "scattered showers" ended and the sun returned.

But torrential rains such as the area had never before seen would continue through most of the night. The result was stark disaster.

The tragic downpour was the result of a freakish meteorological phenomenon that developed over the eastern slopes of the Black Hills. A brisk breeze from the southeast had carried a supply of unusually moist air into the region. When this air collided with the precipitous slopes, it was forced upward to hover over the mountain tops—and the rains began to fall. Usually, precipitation is moved along by air currents, which scatter the rain over large areas. But in this case the high-level winds were weak, and the resulting rainstorms were concentrated completely on the Black Hills and Rapid City.

In six hours, fourteen inches of rain poured down on a small area that usually experienced less than that amount in a year. When it was over, meteorologists differed on measuring the magnitude of the storm, but all agreed that it was an extraordinary event. Some said a deluge of such proportions would not occur more than once in a hundred years; a few insisted that once in several thousand years was a more likely estimate. But the people caught in the great torrent had no time to think of meteorological calculations. Their long night was so filled with horror that once in a million years would have seemed once too often.

In Rapid City the downpour was quite heavy by early evening; still no one felt that there was any danger. But up in the Black Hills, tragedy was already in the making. The prodigious rains quickly turned normally placid mountain streams into raging torrents. Overflows blocked highways and crumbled concrete bridges. Battle Creek, a few miles from Mount Rushmore, and Box Elder Creek, six miles from Rapid City, reached flood stage in a matter of minutes.

Disaster mounted quickly. Campers were drowned in their tents, trailers were overturned by rushing waters, cars were washed away, and homes built along swollen streams collapsed under walls of water. Keystone, an old gold-mining town, was inundated by the rampant waters of Battle Creek. Nine tourists, camped along the banks, were drowned; the camping equipment, cars and belongings of many others were washed downstream. Ron Rathman, who lived on Box

Elder Creek, raced in his car to the aid of an elderly couple who lived along the turgid stream. He never reached his destination; an eight-foot wall of water swept him to his death. A National Guardsman, caught in an overflow, was sucked through a culvert, swept over a 15-foot-high waterfall, and hurled 200 yards downstream where he was smashed against a tree trunk. He was able to hang on until he was rescued.

But the people of Rapid City did not know what was occurring in the Black Hills. They looked through their windows, saw the rain slashing down, allowed as how it was a pretty heavy shower, and returned to their activities. They did not know that the driving rains were but a prelude to the virtual destruction of their pleasant city.

Rapid Creek, from which Rapid City derives its name, is a typical mountain stream, fed by melted snow and rain waters high in the central portion of the Black Hills. Its origin is at 7,140-foot Crooks Tower, 34 miles west of Rapid City, and from this height the waters rush downhill toward Canyon Lake, a 40-acre, man-made pool of water on the edge of one of Rapid City's finest residential areas. In 1972, this neighborhood was protected by a 20-foot-high earthen dam, erected by the WPA in 1938, that permitted enough water through its spillways to allow Rapid Creek to gurgle past the main business district of the city on its way to a junction with the Cheyenne River, 30 miles to the southeast.

It took very little time for the drenching rains to transform Rapid Creek from a bubbling stream to a roaring cataract. In its 34-mile path to the city, the surging creek gathered up houses, chunks of road paving, trailers, trees and other debris and carried all of it downstream. Jerry Mashek, a reporter for the *Rapid City Journal,* said, "We watched in amazement as a small stream spilling from the hillside turned into a four-foot-wide torrent. Rapid Creek, normally clear and placid, sounded like a freight train passing in the night. It must have been 150 feet wide." Harold Higgins, another reporter, viewed the raging creek from a bridge. "I watched a four-foot bank of water come down the stream," he said, "and on top of it a 30-foot house trailer rode the wave like a surfboard." A woman said she saw "a Volkswagen floating down the stream with the people hanging on and screaming for help."

By early evening Rapid Creek was pouring an estimated 30,000 cubic feet of water per-second into Canyon Lake. By nine o'clock the waters of Canyon Lake had risen almost to the crest of the dam, creating a critical situation.

Donald V. Barnett, mayor of Rapid City, was a worried man. He had been receiving disquieting reports from the higher elevations of the Black Hills. A South Dakota State trooper 40 miles west of Rapid City had radioed that the highway he was traveling was under a foot of water. Another patrolman reported a cloudburst on Highway 40, ten miles from Rapid City. Calls indicating that Rapid Creek was overflowing trickled in from various locations.

Shortly after nine P.M., Mayor Barnett heard that the waters of Canyon Lake were lapping at the crest of the dam. He rushed to the area with other officials and a crew of city workers, and by 9:30 they were at the dam attempting to remove debris from the clogged spillway gates. But Mayor Barnett sensed that the situation was hopeless, and by 10 P.M. he withdrew his men from the foot of the dam and ordered police and firemen to alert the people living below the dam to the threat of flood.

At 10:15 the mayor received an emergency call from an unidentified man who said he was eighteen miles from Rapid City and had seen a wall of water roaring down Rapid Creek. "Mr. Mayor," he said, "it looks to me like you've got twenty minutes."

Mayor Barnett immediately called the police department and ordered evacuation of the residences below the dam. He also asked radio station KOTA to advise people owning property adjacent to Rapid Creek to get to higher ground at once.

But it was now too late. The dam crumpled at 10:45, before

most residents could heed the warning, and tons of water cascaded down on the residential neighborhood and then on the business section of Rapid City.

The wall of debris-laden water that poured down on the city was five feet high. Homes in the residential area and stores in the business section crumbled under the onslaught or were swept from their foundations and hurled downstream. Many people had already gone to bed and were awakened only when their homes spun around like tops in the swirling water; they were trapped. Automobiles were picked up and dashed against power pylons or carried along with the flood. Uprooted utility poles were driven through trailers and cars like weapons of war. Gas mains were ruptured and natural gas hissed to the surface. Downed power lines, still alive, ignited the gas, and towering fountains of flame rode the water. Then, suddenly, the city was blacked out as water tore down electrical transmission lines.

Just off Main Street, at the West Side Trailer Court, twenty mobile homes were wiped out. Others went up in flames when fallen power lines ignited propane gas tanks and floated downstream like fiery barges. At another trailer court, 200 mobile homes were swept away; only one remained standing.

The townspeople caught up in the flood and fire fought for their lives. They crawled out on roofs to keep above the waters. They clung to trees, power pylons, light posts. They waded through water and mud, tried to swim, and drowned. One survivor later told a reporter, "Our daughter just floated away. She tried to hold onto a tree but just floated away." It summed up what happened to many of the flood's victims.

Wayne Granum, a fireman, probably had the best view at the moment the dam broke. He was almost sitting on top of it. He had been swept across Canyon Lake on a roof torn from a house and had come to rest among a clump of trees on the edge of the dam. He reached up, grabbed a stout branch, and clung to it desperately. The dam collapsed as he hung there. Granum later described the sight by saying "it was like pulling the plug in a bathtub." The fireman held on to the tree branch until the waters subsided and the roof settled on what was left of the brink of the dam. He finally reached safety, had 30 stitches taken in his lacerated hands, then joined other firemen in rescue work.

Acts of heroism by people who had never before had the opportunity to be heroes were commonplace. Major G. William Medley of Rapid City's Salvation Army left Salvation Army headquarters downtown to aid in the evacuation of people from danger zones around the city. "I've just got to help," he said as he kissed his wife goodbye. He never returned home. His body was found the next morning, half buried in water and muck.

Russ Haley, whose home was directly in the path of the wall of water, did not have time to take his family to safety before the flood arrived. Climbing into a tree alongside his house, he managed to hoist his wife and daughter onto the roof, well above the angry waters. But he found that he could not reach the roof himself. Haley thought fast. He took his belt, hitched himself to a limb of the tree, and hung there for six perilous hours until the flood receded. Later, still able to joke about the experience, he said, "I'm going to leave that belt there as a conversation piece."

Henry Jelkin had a similar adventure. He, his wife and another woman climbed to the roof of their small bungalow and remained there for three hours before being rescued. He said, "You should have seen us three sixty-year-olds perched on the eaves all that time."

Dorrance Dusek, a furniture salesman, noticed a man and his wife stranded in a car. He waded through rapidly moving water to the side of the automobile.

"Take my husband first," the woman said.

Dusek immediately saw her reasoning. Her husband was a

double amputee. Dusek struggled until he had the legless man out of the car, but no sooner had he accomplished this task than the car was swept away by the flood with the woman still inside.

With the crippled man clinging to him, Dusek swam and waded to a nearby house that still seemed sturdy despite the waters swirling around it. But minutes after the two men reached this refuge a wall of the house was torn away and the amputee was carried downstream. Dusek, also swept along by the rushing waters, managed to grab some telephone wires attached to a still-standing house and was later rescued. The amputee and his wife were both drowned.

Gertrude Lux, a frail 71-year-old woman, was trapped in her bedroom with her 16-year-old physically and mentally handicapped granddaughter as the waters rose. Knowing that the girl was not strong enough to stand the waters, which were now chest-high, she placed her on a floating foam-rubber mattress. For five hours the elderly woman stood in the water, holding onto the mattress to keep it from tipping, until she and the girl were rescued the next morning.

Another woman had a similar experience. She held her infant daughter over her head for four hours as she stood in shoulder-deep slime and mud. Both were eventually rescued.

Kerry Conner, a young garage mechanic in a section of town not affected by the flood, drove his truck toward the ruptured dam as soon as he heard about the disaster. On a lawn he spied a rowboat, which he loaded on his truck. He put the rowboat into use when he saw a number of firemen trying to reach people caught in turbulent water. Conner and the firemen worked throughout the night, rescuing at least 25 people. Ironically, Conner was unable to swim, and when his boat was overturned he also had to be pulled from the floodwaters.

Tragedy occurred at the Mountain View Nursing Home

when a wall collapsed and dumped nearly 50 aged patients into the water-filled basement. Patrolman Sam Roach, with the help of several nurses, tied bedsheets together to form ropes and pulled most of the victims from the watery cellar. However, three elderly people died—including one who had already been rescued and decided to go back into the building for her glasses.

Just before the dam broke, Reverend Ronald Masters, anticipating trouble, decided to take his wife, three sons and two daughters to higher ground. He loaded them in his four-wheel-drive utility vehicle and headed for the hills. However, they had gone only a quarter-of-a-mile when the dam burst and a wall of water hit the vehicle. The torrent picked up the automobile and rushed it downstream, "spinning," the minister said, "like a record on a turntable." Eventually the vehicle became wedged among several tall trees.

Reverend Masters knew the water would continue to rise and fill the inside of the car; they would drown unless they could get out. He kicked open a window and managed to squirm out onto the roof of the car. Then he reached over, waving his hand in the window. Grasping his wife's hand, he pulled her up beside him. On his second attempt he caught hold of a foot and pulled out one of his daughters. In her arms was her two-year-old brother, but just as the minister hauled the girl to the top of the car the torrent washed the boy from her and swept him to his death.

Masters had to give up attempts to rescue his other daughter and two sons still trapped in the vehicle because the water had now risen above the car's roof. Sadly, he concluded that they had drowned.

All through a long, torturous night the minister, his wife and daughter stood on the roof of the car and hung onto tree branches to secure themselves. As dawn came the waters began to recede and the roof of their car emerged again. To his surprise the minister heard a strangled cry from within the car. Frantically reaching down through the window, he found a hand and pulled his second daughter from the vehicle, still alive. She had survived by holding her head in a tiny, water-free pocket! However, the two boys inside had drowned.

Shortly after dawn rescue workers in a rowboat reached the family and plucked them from their precarious perch.

Afterward, many bizarre tales were told. One man, clinging desperately to the roof of a house, was surprised to see a white swan swimming by in regal splendor—the only creature of record that seemed to enjoy the rising waters. Four National Guardsmen, trying to reach a submerged car by forming a human chain, with one man solidly anchored to a tree on shore, were swept to their deaths when the tree broke. One family's home was saved from destruction when another house was swept up on their lawn, along with several cars, forming a barrier that broke the force of the floodwaters and directed them elsewhere. A man below the dam watched from his home as the flood tore off the doors to his attached garage and carried his car away. Acting on a hunch that opening the doors of his home might be a way to relieve pressure, he invited the water to flow from the garage, through the house, and out the doors. The house stood up and the only damage was a thick carpet of mud on the floor.

During the long night, rescue attempts continued, but they were hampered by a breakdown in communications. At two A.M. the radio station was knocked off the air and an emergency civil defense band was pressed into service to broadcast instructions to the survivors of the flood. Over and over the same message was repeated: "Stay in your homes and do not impede emergency vehicle traffic. Don't drink the water. Boats are needed immediately. If you find a body, don't touch it. Call . . . "

Not until the light of dawn did many residents of Rapid City realize the severity of damage to their town. By this time the rains had diminished and a murky fog lay over the city. But the wreckage and chaos was plain to see, and it shocked and stunned both those who had survived the brunt of the flood and the fortunate ones who had escaped completely unscathed. Strewn along the lethal path taken by the floodwaters was a jumble of automobiles, ravaged homes, machinery, house trailers, trees—and bodies. One man, weary and smeared with mud, scanned an area across Rapid Creek where his home was located. "I've been through a tornado and I'd say this was five times as bad," he said. "I can't get over there for a close look at my house, but I think my place is still standing, just the way I left it when the water started to rise. But that other mess—looks like I'll never see my neighbor again."

But the city survived. In fact, it is possible that no town ever bounced back from disaster as quickly as Rapid City. By mid-morning of the day following the flood, the local Civil Defense had set up headquarters in the county courthouse. Some 5,000 rescue workers, including 1,800 National Guardsmen who happened to be attending a summer camp nearby, began the tough and tedious work of cleaning up rubbish and locating the bodies of the dead. Rapid City residents who had escaped the flood contributed ten tons of clothing to flood sufferers. Food donations poured in from everywhere, completely filling two hangars at nearby Ellsworth Air Force Base. Young people converged on Rapid City offering their help; many were put to work searching for bodies or directing traffic. Civil Defense authorities later said, "The kids were magnificent."

The Red Cross was on the job quickly, setting up shelters in schools, churches and private homes for the more than 400 homeless. Salvation Army personnel managed kitchens and served 25,000 meals a day. Three temporary morgues were set up and the dead—some so caked with silt and dirt that they had to be hosed down for identification—were placed on concrete slabs while people walked by searching for relatives and friends. The injured were taken to St. John McNamara and Bennet-Clarkson, the city's two major hospitals, and to Ellsworth Air Force Base for treatment. Doctors and nurses worked long hours; the physicians attending the seminar on *Death and the Dying Patient,* offered their services with no thought of reward.

Heavy equipment—bulldozers, cranes, trucks—were donated by contractors from miles around, and 3,000 workers cleared wreckage at a rate of 275 truckloads every hour. A young doctor and his wife, wearing scuba gear, worked underwater to clear intake pipes and get the water system operating again. Medical teams inoculated 20,000 Rapid City residents against tetanus and typhoid. Mayor Barnett, who personally helped in rescue work, ordered all gas service shut off to prevent fires and issued instructions to police to arrest any looters or sightseers with ghoulish intentions.

When President Richard Nixon declared Rapid City a disaster area, a dozen Federal agencies, including the U. S. Army Corps of Engineers, set up emergency headquarters and went to work. In a matter of days, $1,000,000 arrived to aid in recovery.

The search for the dead was the most ghastly task. Little by little the toll mounted—ten at first, then twenty, then a horrendous eighty-five in one ten-block area alone. They were found under water, in half-submerged automobiles, in shattered homes, and under mudslides caused by the rampaging waters. An old woman was found dangling like a puppet from the branches of a tree. Hands and feet stuck up from pools of mud to mark the shallow graves of other victims.

Experienced disaster workers did a noble job, but the people of the city also rolled up their sleeves and helped. Harold Means, a State Highway employee, said "It's unbelievable. Everybody pitched in, giving us more equipment and help than we knew what to do with. I've done construction work all over the world, but I've never seen people like the folks in Rapid City."

Ev Kirschenmann, who ran a small auto repair shop, was a typical example of the spirit that gripped Rapid City after the catastrophe. He was struggling mightily to clear mud and debris from his shop when someone mentioned what a tough job he had on his hands. He smiled and said, "I'm gonna lick it."

Dennis Waltz was another volunteer who stood out among the many. He was helping a National Guard crew, trying to pull a late model car out of a stream bed. The car was mired so deeply that they were having little success. Frustrated, Waltz dropped to his knees and tried hopelessly to clear away mud with his bare hands. "We have to do something," he said. "They tell me a woman and her baby are in this car."

James Montgomery, a National Guardsman, watched Waltz in amazement. "You know," he said reflectively, "this is a terrible thing to be involved in, but since I've been in the Guard this is the first time I've ever felt I was doing something worthwhile."

Stan Rice, a plumbing contractor who lived a mile downstream from the dam, looked at the shambles the flood had made of his $50,000 home. He shrugged and said, "Well, I guess I'll have to move, but living is all an uphill business anyway."

Understandably, there were some who felt helplessly beaten by the flood. One woman, attempting to clean her mud-soaked home, said, "We're down on our hands and knees like animals. I've had enough of the smell of death in this awful, awful mire." A man bemoaned the fact that he had been worth $100,000 before the flood but was now $30,000 in debt because of damage to his house and a group of mobile homes he rented. A woman shoveling mud from her living room picked up the corner of her muddy rug and said with rueful humor, "The salesman said you could wash anything off of it, but I'll bet he wasn't telling the truth.''

As rescue workers labored through piles of trash and explored crumpled homes, many oddities came to light. In a wrecked house that had been knocked off its foundation and swept a dozen yards downstream, a coffee pot still sat upright on the burner of the stove; on the railing of a bridge a sterling silver fruit bowl rested, apparently deposited there by floodwaters; and a home with white walls had a dirty ring around it—like the ring around a bathtub—marking the precise level reached by the flood.

In the wake of tragedy, statistics sound cold and heartless, but they illustrate, perhaps more than anything else, the extent of Rapid City's calamity. The roaring waters of Rapid Creek had carved a path a half-mile wide and thirty miles long through the city. Some 1,200 homes were completely destroyed, another 2,500 badly damaged. One hundred business buildings were demolished. Scattered haphazardly along the path of destruction were 5,000 smashed automobiles, some with people in them. Damage to homes and business places alone stood at more than $31,000,000, and total damage to the city was placed at $100,000,000. And, saddest of all, the death toll was set at 237.

In the final analysis it was the people of Rapid City, guided by such agencies as Civil Defense, Red Cross, Salvation Army and National Guard, who pulled themselves out of the mire. An official of the President's Office of Emergency Preparedness, noting the courage and determination of the people, said, "There's been tremendous generation here. Never before has there been a town that picked itself up and got going again so quickly."

And Mayor Donald Barnett said admiringly, "When I think of how people responded when needed, I am the proudest man in America."

Blizzard!

The U. S. Weather Bureau defines a blizzard as a severe winter snowstorm accompanied by low temperatures and winds of at least 32 miles an hour. Any snowfall that lacks these credentials does not qualify as a true blizzard.

The word blizzard is derived from blast and bluster and came into general use in North America during a particularly frigid winter that numbed the nation in 1880-81. Blizzards occur when the Temperate Zone is invaded by polar winds moving down from Arctic regions. These cold air masses can collide with warm, moist masses from the south, and a violent, wind-driven snowstorm results. Weather forecasters can usually predict such storms and warn people to stay indoors, but blizzards are capricious and may unexpectedly shift direction, burying an unprepared area in tons of snow.

There is more danger inherent in a blizzard than one might think. Thick, swirling clouds of snow reduce visibility to a few feet, and people caught in the white maelstrom can easily lose their sense of direction and become hopelessly lost. Shouting for help in such circumstances is useless, since the sound of a voice is silenced by the continuous roar of the wind.

Many people, blinded by the snow, have frozen to death in a blizzard when they were close to shelter. In farm areas, cattle grazing in the open often succumb before they can be herded to the safety of the barn. In cities, transportation is paralyzed. Deliveries of such critical items as food and heating fuel are halted. Cars, buses and trucks are stranded, trains are bogged down in giant drifts, and airports must be closed.

Blizzards are common in Russia and Canada, less common in the United States. Some of the most severe blizzards this country has faced occurred in 1836, 1863, 1866, 1873, 1888 and, more recently, in 1964. The latter blizzard swept across the northern plains with wind speeds up to 55 miles an hour.

Adelie Land, in the Antarctic, is called the "home of the blizzard" because heavy snow conditions and high winds often persist through the entire winter season. In 1912-13 vicious winds blew down from the ice cap of Antarctica towards the relatively warm sea and resulted in a storm maintaining an average wind velocity of 50 miles an hour, with gusts frequently rising to 100 miles an hour and, on one occasion at least, to 180 miles an hour.

It lasted all winter.

11

The Blizzard That Became a Legend

Northeast U.S.A. (1888)

The Blizzard of '88—like the Johnstown Flood—has become a part of Americana. Like all tales of the weather, the big blizzard has increased in stature, violence and just plain cussedness as the years have passed. Well into the 1950s, elderly survivors with long memories and active imaginations embellished the story of the giant snowstorm that swept the northeastern part of the country and particularly New York City, insisting it was the worst winter storm ever to hit the United States. Some residents of Montana and the Dakotas, where blizzards are more commonplace, questioned the accuracy of this claim from time to time, but they failed to dislodge the storm from the pages of American folklore. The Blizzard of '88 overcame all opposition to nail down its place in history as the one against which all others are measured—and found wanting.

There is no attempt here to tarnish the gaudy reputation of the big winter blow, for it *was* a storm of extreme ferocity. It killed more people than any blizzard ever to strike this country, and it paralyzed the East as no other since. That, to my mind, should be sufficient evidence to support the old-timers who, whenever a heavy snow fell, reminded people that it bore no resemblance whatsoever to "the big storm of '88."

New York City in 1888, with a population of approximately 1,500,000, was the biggest and most congested metropolis in the country. In fact, one-quarter of the population of the United States lived in the northeastern section of the nation, and most of the country's import and export business was channeled through the port of New York. Horsepower, before the advent of the automobile, was not a technical term but a word that expressed exactly what it meant—the number of horses required to pull a loaded wagon. There were horses everywhere: horses hitched to low-slung drays that carried heavy loads; to elegant carriages that transported the wealthy set to soirees and the theater; and to horsecars that, despite the fact that New York had built its first elevated railroad line in the 1880s, still carried most of the working people of the city to and from their places of employment.

New York bustled incessantly. Then, as now, Wall Street was the financial center of the city and the frenetic Stock Exchange was a place where people who didn't own stock went to watch the peculiar antics of those who did. Trains rumbled in and out of Grand Central Depot, and in New York harbor, little tugs darted about like beetles, puffing importantly as they nudged ocean liners and heavily-laden freighters into their berths. Central Park was a green oasis in a dingy city, where fine young ladies wearing ankle-length skirts and carrying parasols could stroll with their admiring swains. And Broadway, even then, was the show-biz street, where the latest plays drew large crowds.

On Sunday, March 11, 1888—the day the blizzard started with an innocent-appearing morning rain—New Yorkers had other concerns than the weather on their minds. Spring was just around the corner, and already farmers on Long Island were thinking about early crops while Manhattan-dwellers were pondering what flowers to plant in their window boxes or limited plots of ground. Children were in their annual state of excitement because Barnum and Bailey's circus was appearing at Madison Square Garden, and their fathers were wondering if the New York Giants, who were looking good in spring training, could really win the National League pennant that year. Broadway glittered with some of the best productions of the season; Daly's Theater was presenting a play which had, in view of what was about to happen, the most inappropriate title in town—*A Midsummer Night's Dream*.

What hit the city on the evening of March 11 was more like a midwinter night's nightmare.

The big storm came as a surprise to everyone, including the weather bureau, which had predicted cooler weather and light snow. The scant morning rain was nothing to get excited over, and even when the rain became a heavy downpour on Sunday afternoon it presented no cause for alarm. Since Monday was a working day, people went to bed early and listened to the falling rain on their roofs before dropping off to sleep. When they awoke the next morning the scene around them had changed. The rain had turned to snow during the night, and people reluctantly resigned themselves to putting on winter boots and overcoats for one more bout with winter.

The meteorological explanation for the unexpected snowstorm was a simple one. During the night there had been a collision of weather fronts. From the region of the Great Lakes a cold front carrying gale winds and swirling snow had swept across New York State to the coast. At the same time heavy winds and rains moved up from Georgia to meet the cold front from the northwest. The two storms clashed, and the result was a sharp drop in temperatures and a blinding snowstorm that began at about 11 P.M. on Sunday, March 11. By Monday morning, when the heads of households were preparing to go to work, the snow was already two feet deep in most places, with drifts up to five feet. By noon on Monday, the accumulation reached a depth of five feet in the lowest places, with drifts up to eighteen feet.

Surprised at the sudden snow but uncowed by it, most men started for work. Some got there and others didn't. Many waited on corners for horsecars that never came. Others walked to work, trudging through knee-deep snow while half blinded by the world of white around them. During that morning, winds swept across New York City at eighty-four miles an hour, and the temperature plummeted to four degrees below zero.

It wasn't long before those who had ventured outside began to realize that this storm was the biggest and most severe they had ever encountered.

One of the more intrepid New Yorkers to brave the big storm was Charlie Jones, who had an office in lower Manhattan on Wall Street. Six months before the storm he had vowed to walk to work from his uptown home and back again for a year. On Monday morning he started out as usual for his office, staggering through trackless snow and hunched against the gale winds and below zero temperatures. Before long he realized that walking to work on this particular morning was not the smartest thing he had ever done, but he kept on until he finally entered the warmth of his office. That evening Jones had a dinner engagement at Delmonico's in upper Manhattan and one might have excused him if he refused to set out on foot again. But he stubbornly threw caution to the winds and arrived at the restaurant red-faced, weary and, it must be assumed, proud of himself.

Another man, whose name does not survive, proved just as

determined. He ascended to the 50th Street station of the Sixth Avenue elevated, planning to take the car to his job at the City Hall. A ticket-seller turned him away, explaining that the cars were not running.

"How do I get to City Hall?" the man asked.

The ticket-seller shrugged. "Walk, I guess."

Disgruntled, the man descended and flagged down a passing, two-horse cab.

"Hi, cabbie—are you engaged?" he asked.

"No," the driver said, "and I don't want to be."

"I'll give you five dollars to carry me to City Hall."

"Not for twenty-five," the cabbie said. "I'll be in luck if I get my team to the stable. In fact, I'm in luck right now just to be alive."

There was nothing left to do but walk and, bracing his body once more against the howling winds, the man stumbled as far as 42nd Street. At that point he saw an expressman hauling four trunks on a sled and asked for a ride.

"It'll cost you a dollar a block," the expressman said.

"I don't want to *buy* your team," the man snorted and, pulling his coat collar up around his neck, again walked against the wind. At 29th Street he stopped to extract an exhausted young girl from a snowdrift, then carried her to a hotel where she could recuperate. That accomplished, he set out on his journey again.

A few blocks farther on a policeman grabbed him. Before the man knew what was happening, his face was being rubbed with snow. "Your ear is frozen," the policeman said. "Better get inside now, mister."

The man thanked his benefactor but continued on until he finally reached City Hall. It had taken him four hours to make the trip.

However, most workers who started out on foot for their places of business lacked such raw determination. Hundreds walked a block or two and turned back. Some were actually blinded by the blizzard and became lost. Those who did reach their shops or offices found them virtually deserted. No business was being transacted. Telephone and telegraph wires were down. The trains were stalled. Mail was not being delivered. Food deliveries into the city were halted. Stores and restaurants were closed because employees could not reach them. Travelers were marooned in hotels. Isolated in their offices, workers looked out on deserted streets. The relentless snow was so heavy that nearby buildings were blotted out; nothing moved below—not a wagon, not a carriage, not a person. Bustling, restless New York City had come to a standstill.

Unknown to New Yorkers, the same situation prevailed in other eastern cities. Boston was snowed in. Philadelphia was buried. The business of government in Washington was halted. In between the major cities, small towns were isolated. Nothing south of Maine or north of Virginia moved. Paralysis extended from the East Coast to Buffalo.

Trains were in particularly dire straits. Those attempting to reach New York City were stalled in monstrous snowdrifts in upstate New York, Pennsylvania and the New England states. Outgoing trains that had left New York late Sunday were similarly bogged down. Passengers were worried. Food for the dining cars ran low and finally was gone. Engines ran out of coal and the cars became dreary iceboxes. The passengers asked anxiously when they would be able to go on. Nobody knew.

Ships at sea were endangered. Several ocean-going liners were due to arrive in New York Monday morning, but they rode out the storm at sea rather than risk coming into the narrow confines of New York harbor. Pilot boats and tugs off the Battery bounced around like corks in the windswept waters or were splintered against pilings at dockside. Two pilot boats sank with all hands. Off the coast of Delaware, fifteen boats were missing; in Chesapeake Bay almost a hundred vessels were sunk or wrecked; in Delaware Bay, 37 boats were demolished, and in New York Bay the toll was 33.

Pilot Boat No. 13 was caught in Monday's hurricane-like winds near Sandy Hook. On board was William Inglis, a reporter for the *New York World,* who planned to do a story about life on a pilot boat. He couldn't have chosen a worse day. The ocean became so rough that the boat almost capsized on several occasions, and Inglis was not only seasick but sick of the whole assignment. Time after time, when it seemed the ship would sink, the plucky little vessel would right itself again. Battered and leaking, the pilot boat survived a terrifying 24 hours before it was finally able to make port. Inglis had a different story to write than the one he had planned on.

On land the pile-up of snow devastated communities throughout the East. In Massachusetts, drifts towered 40 feet high. Hew Haven, Connecticut, claimed one drift of 53 feet. Pittsfield, Massachusetts, was interred in 20 feet of snow, with some houses completely covered.

During the height of the storm the New York City Weather Bureau anemometer was knocked out. The bureau wanted badly to record this most violent of all storms, but fixing the wind gauge in such weather seemed an impossibility. The gauge was stationed on a pole atop the Equitable Building, 150 feet above the street, and it would be suicidal for anyone to attempt to reach it. But finally Francis Long, who had been a member of Adolphus Greely's expedition to the Arctic, volunteered to fix the gauge. Long shinnied up the thin pole, which was actually bending in the wind, and made the necessary adjustments to the recorder.

By noon those few businesses that had opened closed down, either sending their employees home or inviting them to stay through the night. Salesgirls and clerks in several department stores spent the night sleeping on bedding issued to them by their employers. Hotels were jammed with men who sought rooms for the night rather than risk a journey home; many of them had to sleep in the lobbies and hallways. Bars did a land office business—until they ran out of liquor. Many business men, reluctant to venture out even for dinner, slept in their offices.

The Stock Exchange suspended business at noon when only 30 out of 1,100 members showed up. Courts were adjourned when judges and juries were unable to appear. Grocery stores, unable to get produce, closed their doors. The few that remained open had no customers. But on Broadway three theaters honored the tradition that "the show must go on" and gave their evening performances before only a handful of people. And at Madison Square Garden, Barnum and Bailey's circus put on both matinee and evening performances before barely a hundred spectators.

In rural areas, farmers had duties to perform despite the cold and snow. Livestock had to be fed and cows milked, and the farmers fought the blizzard to perform these essential chores. Most succeeded, but one Long Island farmer battled through snowdrifts to reach his barn, then became lost in the blinding blizzard on his way back to the house. Exhausted, he stumbled into a snowdrift and froze to death.

Many strange incidents occurred during the big blow. One man, attempting to walk home from his office, became exhausted and leaned wearily against a lamp post for support. Before he had recovered enough strength to go on, he fell asleep, with the side of his face against the metal pole. The whistling winds and low temperature caused his face to freeze against the post and he awoke with a start. Painfully, he disengaged his jaw from the pole and, realizing that he could have frozen to death, he called on his last ounce of energy and plodded homeward. When he reached his house he went to bed immediately and slept the sleep of the exhausted.

Waking in the morning, the man realized for the first time that his false teeth were gone. Thinking back over the previous day's hard experience, he decided that the only place he could have lost them was at the lamp post. Since the storm had abated somewhat, he went back to the scene and found his teeth frozen to the metal pole.

The danger of falling asleep during the blizzard also was exemplified by John Paultz, a delivery man. He set out in the morning with his horse and wagon to deliver meat to stores on his route. Trying to warm himself against the bitter cold, he took several man-sized swigs of whiskey along the way. He had not gone far when drowsiness overtook him, and he pulled his wagon to the side of the street and went to sleep. If it had not been for the intervention of an alert policeman, both Paultz and his horse would have perished. The policeman dragged Paultz from the wagon and rubbed his face with snow, then took him inside a building to revive him. Paultz later said, "When I fell asleep I was very comfortable and I thought I was home."

In Yonkers, C. H. McDonald stumbled into a deep snowdrift and hit his head on a hard object, opening an ugly gash in his forehead. Searching around, he found that his head had hit the hoof of a dead horse buried in the snow. McDonald's sense of humor came to the fore, and he spent several days showing people his wound and claiming to be the only man in New York ever to have been kicked by a dead horse.

A more tragic fate befell Senator Roscoe Conkling, who attempted to walk to the New York Club from his Wall Street office. Slogging through the deep snow at Union Square, he soon found himself trapped in a huge snowdrift. For nearly half an hour the Senator struggled to free himself, and for most of that time he doubted his ability to escape the drift. But finally he made it and stumbled on through the snow and heavy winds until he came to the club. By that time he was covered with snow and ice and his clothing was practically frozen to his body. It had taken three bitter hours to complete his walk. Exhausted and weak, he lay in bed the next day suffering delirium and died a short time later of overexertion.

Walking across the five-year-old Brooklyn bridge was a daily feat for people who lived on one side and worked on the other. But not on the morning of the blizzard. Several men attempted it but had to turn back after going a short distance. The winds over the bridge were of hurricane force, and crossing the high arch became so dangerous that the police closed the span to pedestrians. But a foolhardy young bank clerk with a persuasive tongue talked the police into letting him try it. He explained that he had important business in Manhattan and it was absolutely necessary for him to get there. Besides, he was young and strong and he would be able to make it without difficulty.

Reluctantly the police let him go, but watched him carefully as he started across the bridge. It turned out to be more than the bank clerk had bargained for, and he got less than halfway across before he collapsed under the onslaught of the piercing winds and swirling snow. The police managed to rescue him and bring him back to the Brooklyn side, where they rushed him to a hospital. He was badly frostbitten.

A milkman in lower Manhattan was determined to make his deliveries despite the snowstorm. Facing the sting of wind-driven snow, he plodded through giant drifts to bring milk to his customers. All at once a snowdrift gave way beneath him, and he sank five or six feet. But he wasn't buried. Instead he had stumbled into a tunnel dug beneath the drift by two boys who were digging their way out of a store. The milkman still clutched in his hand the quart of milk he was carrying when he dropped into the tunnel. Laughing at his experience, he took a shovel and helped the boys dig themselves out to the street.

On Long Island an inventive young lad went shopping for his mother on a pair of homemade snowshoes. In the process he walked past the tops of tall trees over drifts that he estimated at 60 feet.

By Monday evening most people had either holed up in hotels and offices or made it safely back to their homes. But the howling blizzard still raged, dumping more and more snow on the stricken Northeast. By mid-morning Tuesday the blizzard began to abate and people emerged from their homes like moles to inspect the damage. The weather bureau in New York officially measured the depth of the snow at 20.9 inches, a record fall, but this did not take into consideration the mountainous wind-blown drifts that blocked entrances to buildings and homes and made movement in the city virtually impossible for days.

But the dying blizzard had one more devious trick to play on its human victims. A giant ice floe in New York harbor rode in on the tide and wedged itself in the East River, forming a hazardous and slippery bridge between Brooklyn and Manhattan. Hundreds of men congregated on a Brooklyn dock, gazing at the strange sight and wondering if it might be possible to cross over the East River on foot. But no one had the courage to try it.

Finally a fourteen-year-old boy with a shrewd business sense came upon the scene with a ladder and invited the men to descend from the dock to the sheet of ice for two cents each. A few adventurous souls took him up on the offer, followed by a dozen more, and eventually a flood of humanity, all anxious to "walk to Manhattan," started out over the ice. The ice proved firm and hundreds made the crossing.

However, the Brooklyn police took a dim view of this foolhardiness. Knowing that the ice would break up when high tide was reached and the water began to ebb, they formed a human barrier along the dock and refused to let people cross. But they arrived too late to prevent a potential tragedy. Five men were caught on the ice floe when it started to float back to the harbor. As it floated away, huge chunks began to break off at its edges.

Like the cavalry in an old western movie that arrives just in time to rescue the hero from the Indians, a tugboat came up the river at the crucial moment. The tug managed to smash its way through the churning ice and pluck the men off the floe before it disintegrated.

Wednesday became a day of deliverance. The snow stopped. The winds died down. All over New England, as in New York City, snow removal efforts began. Individuals dug their homes out of the powdery whiteness; city crews moved into action, clearing streets and attacking stubborn snow-drifts. People who had been in the doldrums through two days of storm began to once more exhibit a sense of humor. One man, finding a fifteen-foot-high drift in front of his house, put a sign on the snow pile: THIS SNOW FOR SALE. Another facetiously placed a notice on a snowdrift that said: LOST IN THIS PILE OF SNOW, A VALUABLE DIAMOND. FINDER MAY KEEP IT.

Slowly, gradually, normal life resumed. Stranded trains began to move. Telegraph and telephone lines were repaired and service restored. Stores and other business places re-opened their doors and food deliveries once more began to make their way into the cities. Tugboats and pilot boats began to steam about New York harbor, bringing in the ocean liners and freighters that had suffered through the blizzard at sea.

As the eastern section of the country recovered, the destruction and loss of life wrought by the blizzard became known. Four hundred people, two hundred in New York City alone, died in the great storm. New York City estimated damage at $20,000,000. All along the East Coast, north from Chesapeake Bay, the storm left a tangled heap of wrecked ships and docks. Some 200 boats were sunk, or blown onto dry land and ripped apart by winds. In outlying areas, hundreds of horses and cattle were found frozen to death. Thousands of birds and small animals died. Snowdrifts were so deep in some places that people claimed they failed to melt completely until June or July.

Not long after the storm, a group of men formed a club, calling themselves The Blizzard Men of '88. To join this clique, one had to be a bonafide survivor of the big blow. For many years the group met annually for lunch, trading stories and experiences that undoubtedly grew more exciting with each telling. Each time New York City suffered a heavy snowfall that younger people claimed was just as great, or greater, than the Blizzard of '88, the Blizzard Men stoutly maintained that it was not. Then, on December 26, 1947, New York received the greatest snowfall in its history—a record 25.8 inches. That exceeded the snowfall of '88 by 4.9 inches, and at last a new generation of New Yorkers had solid ammunition with which to attack the claims of those Blizzard Men of '88 still on the scene.

New York's newspapers and magazines labeled the 1947 storm the greatest blizzard of all time, taking great delight in finally puncturing the boastful claims made for the '88 storm. But then came a cruel blow. The New York Weather Bureau announced that while the 1947 snowfall was the deepest on record, the storm had no accompanying winds and therefore could not be classified as a blizzard at all!

The Blizzard Men had won another round and, although there may not be any of them left today to relish the victory, the Blizzard of '88 still stands as the deadliest and most destructive on this continent—and the one that remains as an unperishable part of American history.

Tornado!

The tornado—often called a twister—is one of the most vicious and destructive storms on earth. It is capable of demolishing a town in a matter of minutes, leaving total devastation in its wake.

Simply described, the tornado is a violent, twisting windstorm that has the appearance of a giant funnel, with the narrow end pointing toward the earth. It is usually born several thousand feet above the ground, and it extends downward from a black mass of cumulo-nimbus clouds. The funnel, spinning like a top, may never reach the earth at all, in which case it does no damage. But the unpredictable behavior of the storm may cause it to dip down suddenly and bounce along the ground, causing unimaginable destruction.

Most tornadoes have short lives. Few twisters are wider than 300 yards across and they normally cut a swath no longer than 15 or 16 miles. They move along at speeds between 25 and 40 miles an hour, and the rotating winds inside the funnel reach a savage 300 miles an hour or more. Tornadoes form when moist warm air moves up from the south to meet cold air from the north. The cold air sinks, the warm air rises, and air rushes in from all directions to replace the rising warm air. This inrushing air begins to rotate, and the hideous black funnel is born.

A tornado can destroy in three specific ways. First, the violent rotating winds on the edges of the tornadic funnel can blow down trees and buildings. Second, the center of the vortex can explode houses by causing an extreme drop in air pressure on the outside of a building. When the air inside is unable to escape in time to equalize pressure on the walls and roof, the structure simply blows up. Third, there is a strong updraft in the funnel that sucks up trees, houses, automobiles and other heavy material. Sometimes the twister will carry such debris for miles before dropping it back to earth.

Tornadoes have occurred in Canada, Asia, Africa, Australia and New Zealand, but most of them strike the midwest United States. The United States National Weather Service records show that the most vulnerable states are Kansas, Iowa, Texas, Oklahoma, Arkansas, Missouri, Alabama and Mississippi.

If you live in tornado country, you know what a twister looks like. If you don't, you should know what to look for. Most tornadoes occur on warm, sultry afternoons when black clouds begin to form and a thunderstorm seems imminent. A whirling mass forms under one of the clouds and stretches downward to shape the funnel, which, in this country, usually begins to travel in a northeasterly direction. That's when to take cover. Assuming that you have no storm cellar, the safest place is the southwest portion of your house—in the basement, or, if you have no basement, under a table or bed. Rubble from a collapsed home usually is deposited in the northeast corner. If caught in the open it's best to lie in a ditch flat on the ground.

12

America's Deadliest Tornado
Midwest U.S.A. (1925)

March 18, 1925 was a warm and muggy day throughout America's Midwest. Missouri, Illinois and Indiana sweltered under a broiling sun, but few residents of these states complained. The warmth, considered a harbinger of spring, convinced the people that the long-awaited relief from winter's icy grip was close at hand. Even the weather prediction for the area—thunderstorms late in the day—was welcomed. The rains should end the sticky heat and bring about an even better day on the morrow.

If anyone took note of the fact that spring regularly ushered in the "tornado season" in the central states of the nation, it must have been put quickly out of mind. Midwesterners hoped that the "twisters" would stay away if one simply denied their existence, in the same way that those living in earthquake-prone California ignore the fact that disaster is as near as the next tick of the clock.

In any attack—whether by the forces of nature or man's

instruments of war—the element of surprise inevitably increases damage and loss of life. This is what happened when the great killer-tornado danced across the Ohio Valley on the afternoon of March 18. No one expected it. No one was prepared. And no one in the path of the giant-sized twister escaped unscathed, suffering, at the very least, the fright of a lifetime.

Before its deadly work was completed, the tornado traveled 300 miles in five horrendous hours; devastated more than 30 towns, totally destroying half a dozen of them; claimed the lives of 689 people; injured an estimated 3,000; demolished property to the tune of $17,000,000; and took its place in the annals of historic storms as the greatest single tornado ever to ravage the Midwest.

Although Professor Henry J. Cox, government forecaster at Chicago, later described the tornado as "a typical middlewest springtime storm," it traveled farther and did damage over a greater area than most. The twister was born over the Gulf of California, passed harmlessly over several southeastern states, took its first dip toward earth in Arkansas, and then followed the path of least resistance along the Ohio Valley. It struck first in southeastern Missouri, then jumped the Mississippi River into southern Illinois. In the Prairie State it battered one town after another, then skipped into Indiana to lay waste to the southwest tip of the Hoosier State. Having by this time spent its major force, the tornado rode off in a northeasterly direction on high winds that kept it elevated. Although rated as a single tornado, the twister that roared through the Ohio Valley spawned several spin-offs, one of which reached into Kentucky and Tennessee.

Annapolis, Missouri, a sleepy town of approximately 200 people, was first on the tornado's long list of victims. Shortly after one P.M., while clouds blackened overhead and occasional streaks of lightning split the sky, the Tri-State Tornado, as it came to be known, whirled down upon the tiny

Ozark hamlet. It pranced down the main street, shattering every building in its path but three, and hurling the wreckage it created up a hillside. Miraculously, only two people were killed in Annapolis, but many were injured—most of them receiving broken arms or legs from flying debris. Property damage in the tiny town reached half a million dollars.

W. C. Gunther, station agent at the Missouri Pacific depot in Annapolis, was one of those who had a lucky escape. He was sitting at his desk in the station's bay window when the funnel roared in and collapsed most of the station around him. By some trick of the wind, the timbers supporting the window remained upright, and Gunther was left unhurt in the only undamaged section of the depot. Meanwhile, in the waiting room, several persons were pinned beneath falling timbers, and when a portion of the station caught fire, a quick-thinking clerk used his cash drawer as a bucket to extinguish the flames.

Three other Missouri towns—Biehle, Altenburg and Cape Girardeau—were heavily damaged, but again there were comparatively few casualties. A school at Cape Girardeau was swept off its foundation and carried away—just after the pupils had been released for the day.

It was in southern Illinois that the tornado did its worst. There the spinning storm raced through Murphysboro, De-Soto, West Frankfort and a dozen other towns, strewing hundreds of dead in its path.

Murphysboro, located near the Mississippi River in the heart of a dairy farming and fruit growing district, suffered the most. Whirling down upon the west end of the city of 11,000 with the grinding noise of a freight train, the tornado crumpled buildings, tossed houses into the air, snapped telephone poles, uprooted giant trees, burst water mains, sucked up debris and spun it around in the air, all in a few minutes. People were crushed by falling buildings or died in their demolished homes. Some were lifted bodily and carried along by the raging twister, then slammed against the sides of buildings or hurled violently to the ground. Those who survived these terrifying minutes owed their lives to luck as much as anything else, for the tornado picked its victims at random. To add to the horror, debris scattered by the twister caught fire, and flames raged through the town for hours afterward, devouring still-living victims trapped in the wreckage. When the tornado had passed, firefighters found the water works in ruins and had to improvise a pumping plant. The wreckage left by the twister included the Mobile and Ohio Company, a $25,000 Baptist church, and a new $267,000 addition to the high school.

Several freakish things occurred in Murphysboro. The tornado ripped the wall off of an apartment building and exposed a kitchen but disturbed neither the furniture nor the dishes on the table. The top of a house was torn off and carried away by the twister, leaving the first floor intact, with the floor of the second story serving as a roof. On the second floor, exposed to the elements after the tornado passed, was a bed, its bedspread hardly wrinkled. In another case, a two-by-four was driven through the trunk of a tree. This example of nature's handiwork can be seen today in an Illinois museum.

One of the strangest cases was that of the Reverend H. W. Abbot, pastor of the First Baptist Church, who left a stack of 500 calling cards lying on a bookcase in his study. When the tornado struck his house, it sucked up the cards and carried them off. One of them was found later in Palestine, Illinois, 210 miles away.

Charles Biggs, a laborer, was in his automobile when he saw the ominous funnel-shaped cloud approaching Murphysboro. Recognizing it for what it was, he leaped from the car and took refuge in a ditch.

"I saw the car turn over several times and then I never saw

it again," Biggs said later. "I walked the rest of the way home, a mile and a half. The place was a complete wreck. I saw my daughter-in-law sitting, dazed, and she died while I tried to talk to her. Her two daughters were 25 feet away, dead. My wife and mother were there, too—dead. Nearby was my 21-year-old son, Fred—he was dead. Near him was my daughter, Margaret—she was sixteen years old just two days ago—and she was dead. My other daughter, at school, was the only one saved. I was only scratched."

Seven-year-old Agnes Price was in her home when the tornado hit. With her was Mrs. I. H. Perkins, wife of a minister. When the hideous noise of the tornado was heard and the walls of the house began to tremble, Agnes fell to her knees and prayed, saying, "Oh, Lord, I ain't saved and I've been a sinner." The Lord must have heard her plea, for she escaped uninjured.

So tremendous were the violently rotating winds of the tornado that eleven locomotives were tipped over and wrecked. Heavy debris was later found several miles from the city, and papers were carried fifty miles.

Murphysboro suffered 210 dead and more than 500 injured, giving the town the dubious distinction of being the hardest hit community of all.

But the Tri-State Tornado wasn't finished. DeSoto, Illinois, a small town of about 600 residents, was wiped off the map in the blinking of an eye. The revolving funnel ripped through the town, scattering wreckage right and left. Frame homes were torn apart, brick houses crumbled. Every business building was demolished and within seconds no structure more than ten feet high was left standing. So fierce was the wind that bodies of DeSoto residents were found in fields a mile away, and timbers from the wrecked town were found in Duquoin, fifteen miles away.

F. M. Hewitt, former state senator from nearby Carbondale, was in DeSoto the day of the tornado and later gave a detailed description of his experiences:

> I was with T. L. Cherry, a friend [he said] in the home of a DeSoto woman to transact some business. The lady was showing us her six-week-old twins when we saw the clouds looming on the horizon. We went outside and saw big boiling clouds... with a funnel-shaped black center. I said that I believed it was a tornado and we went to the home of a woman across the street who came out carrying a baby to watch the phenomenon.
>
> We could see that it was coming nearer and on the horizon, through intermittent flashes of lightning, could see timbers and other debris which seemed to be floating in the air on the crest of the wind. I advised against going inside, but we all finally went into the home of the neighbor.
>
> The wind increased to the roar of a tremendous draft which sounded like a lumbering wagon coming down the street. Suddenly the house we were in was lifted about ten feet and moved through the air, settling about twenty feet distant. We then got outside as fast as we could.
>
> Cherry was knocked unconscious by a flying timber. I felt like I was going to fly and was being drawn straight up into the air. Then I fell down. I saw a post nearby and thought if I could get to it I would not be sucked into the air. I finally crawled to it and held tight.
>
> I felt rather foolish and wondered what people would think if they saw me lying flat on the ground and holding fast to a fence post. But as I looked I could see houses and other buildings lifted into the air in a mass and then could see them disintegrate.
>
> After it was over I remember first hearing the cries of babies everywhere and then of frantic mothers searching for their children. I got to my feet and looked around. It seemed to me that bodies were everywhere, particularly the bodies of old people and children. Some of them were red with blood and some of them had all their clothing torn off.
>
> I tried to help the women hunting for their children. Then I heard the screaming of the injured. I would go to one person and start elsewhere to get help for him, only to find another

person more desperately hurt. Then I would hear another cry and find another still more seriously injured. I never returned to the same person twice.

It seemed that I was the only person alive and I was short of breath. I wondered if I was the only one to escape the tornado, only to die of suffocation. Then I saw a neighbor who had been a short distance away. It seemed to me he and I were the only persons left and I felt that he was the only friend I had in the world and didn't want to lose sight of him. We started pulling out the dead and injured from the wrecked homes and then others came to help. Later I found that the woman and her twins had escaped.

One of the most horrifying incidents was the destruction of the DeSoto public school. One hundred-and-twenty-five children and teachers were there when the tornado tore the top story off and sailed it away like a giant kite. As a result the lower walls caved in, burying the pupils in rubble. Later, 88 bodies were pulled from the wreckage.

Max Burton, a telegraph operator for the Illinois Central Railroad in Tamaroa, rushed to DeSoto as soon as he heard of the disaster. He later described the town as a "mass of bodies, maimed residents, debris and burning buildings."

> It seemed to me [he said] that there was not an entire house in the town. People were going out on the hard road, north and south, with a few belongings clutched in their arms, more for protection against the storm than anything else, so far as I could see.
>
> I went directly to the school house, after running and walking two-and-a-half miles, and the first thing I saw were the bodies of about twenty-five children laid out on mattresses and blankets. There was no one there to claim them, so I thought the people I had seen on the hard road were their parents. But I learned later that the children's parents had been killed or wounded and those who were not dead were being hurried by automobile, special relief train and ambulances to the hospitals at Carbondale and Duquoin.
>
> The principal of the school was on hand and he was trying to

identify the bodies of the people and was also worrying over the whereabouts and safety of two girl teachers who were unaccounted for. The principal was bloody from his own injuries and staggered in his walk. He had barely escaped with his life.

The bodies of the school children were piled up just outside the playgrounds and they were still seeking others in the ruins. While I stood there they took some of the bodies away and brought others out of the building, which by then was a mass of smoldering ruins, fire having destroyed what the tornado had not. The hallway of the building had caved in and what few rescuers were on hand were trying to uncover other bodies of pupils and locate the two missing teachers.

I walked out beyond the school grounds and near the city limits I saw the bodies of two babies, apparently about six- or eight-months-old. They were dead and their baby clothes had been torn from them. Every tree that was left standing and every fence had garments, bed clothes and household goods blown against the west side of them. It looked to me as if the tornado began in the west and traveled eastward. I saw furniture, automobile tops and clothing scattered everywhere and saw many people fleeing from the town with hardly any garments.

The business district was practically destroyed by fire and wind and nearly every home was flat. I saw about 40 automobiles piled up in one big heap and figured this was a garage that had been struck. Then I saw another car just outside of town that looked like the people were trying to get away, but had failed. The car had been blown from the road over to the railroad right-of-way and was wrecked, but I could find no bodies. Automobiles were stretched along the hard roads north and south of DeSoto for nearly three miles.

I offered what help I could and they told me that the dead and injured were first taken to Carbondale, but that the hospital there was filled and they were taking them to Duquoin hospital, north of DeSoto.

The fire departments of Duquoin and Carbondale were sent to DeSoto, but they were unable to do anything and the firemen pitched in to do rescue work. I could see them digging the bodies out of the school house and other buildings.

> I saw two girls on the hard road on my way back home. Their faces were bleeding and their clothes were torn. I figured they had escaped from the school. One of them said, "How did you get out?" and the other answered, "I climbed out the window. How did you get out?" The first one said, "I don't even know." They were wandering up the road and seemed not to know where they were going.

Jesse Pankey, driving to his home from St. Louis with his wife and two small children, saw the funnel approaching and drove into a garage to escape. He got out of the car just in time to see the roof of the garage whirled away. Then, to his horror, the car, with his wife and two children still in it, was tossed into the air and carried off.

Pankey had hardly recovered from this shock when he was lifted bodily and swept through the air for five blocks. The tornado set him down again gently on the Illinois Central Railroad tracks. Fortunately, he found his wife and children in a plowed field, only slightly injured.

Another bit of good luck saved a young mother who was lying in bed with her two-week-old baby when the tornado collapsed her home. Timbers came crashing down toward the bed, but they formed a tent over the mother and her child, protecting them from injury.

DeSoto, ravaged by the twister and finished off by fire, was almost completely destroyed. The death toll was 118, with 200 injured.

The coal mining community of West Frankfort (population about 12,000) was another southern Illinois town that took sledge-hammer blows from the tornado. One-third of the residential section was wiped out, and the Orient Mine, one of the city's chief sources of livelihood, was wrecked. Within a minute or two, the ferocious twister reduced the areas it struck to tangled debris. Houses were torn apart, light and telephone poles downed, trees uprooted. During its cruel attack the roar of the tornado was deafening, and as soon as it had passed a weird unearthly silence fell over the stricken town. People who had escaped alive came out of their damaged homes to survey the carnage. Many others lay dead in the twisted wreckage.

The scene was unbelievable. Some homes that were still in good repair had been moved off their foundations by the powerful winds. Others stood with one wall ripped off, revealing neatly arranged furniture still in place. Most dwellings lay totally wrecked in a heap of lumber and bricks.

Bodies were scattered haphazardly in the streets, and the cries and screams of the injured, pinned beneath the debris, began to break the deadly silence. Rescue work began. In one pile of rubble a young mother lay terribly mangled while her baby crawled around nearby, crying lustily. One woman was found on her front porch, a jagged wound on her forehead; the tornado had cut her down as she attempted to flee. A dazed man stumbled around in the wreckage of his house, holding the limp form of a five-year-old in his arms. He was searching for the rest of his family. He found them—his wife and another son—badly injured.

A young woman, half buried in the debris of her home, was crying with pain, but when rescue workers approached her she pointed to another pile of rubble nearby.

"Don't bother with me," she gasped. "Get my baby out!"

The workers found a five-day-old boy in the ruins, unhurt. They took him out gently and then freed the woman.

Frank Bell, his wife and two sons, were in their small frame home when the twister dipped down on the town. "We just hung onto the table," Bell said afterward. "The house was lifted off its foundation and bumped down again. We were not hurt."

The capricious tornado attacked certain objects and left others nearby untouched. A frame building of the West Frankfort water plant was undamaged, while large trees all around it were snapped off or uprooted. Hundreds of automobiles, most with their tops ripped off, were turned over and scattered along the streets. Just outside of town, on the West Frankfort-Benton highway, was a tin-can dump. The entire pile of cans was picked up and deposited on the opposite side of the road. A barber's chair was found sitting upright in a field near West Frankfort, apparently carried out of town and planted there by tricky winds.

Humor occasionally mingled with tragedy. The *West Frankfort Daily American,* determined not to let a tornado halt its presses, put out an extra issue the evening of the storm. One newsboy failed to show up to hustle papers out to customers. When the circulation manager learned that the boy was unhurt, he asked him why he hadn't shown up to deliver his papers.

"How can I?" the youngster demanded. "My route's all blown away."

Statistics for West Frankfort were numbing: 107 dead, 500 injured, 250 buildings leveled, property damage estimated at $2,000,000.

Other southern Illinois towns felt the fury of the tornado, although casualty figures were not as great. Stricken towns included Gorham, McLeansboro, Parrish, Logan, Benton, Enfield, Bush, Thomsonville, Carmi, Crossville and Akin. Having dealt with these, the tornado crossed into Indiana, where it ravaged Princeton, Owensville, Griffin, Poseyville and Elizabeth. Princeton, with a population of 7,000, was hard hit, suffering 20 deaths and 200 injuries. Nearly every building and business in the southern part of the town was leveled, including the $2,000,000 Southern Railroad facilities and the Heinz pickle factory, recently built at a cost of a million-and-a-half dollars. Despite the destruction of the Heinz plant, all but one of the 75 women employed there escaped injury—another miracle in the midst of disaster.

There were the usual number of lucky escapes. T. H. Phillips was sitting in the office of his coal scale shop alongside the Southern Railroad tracks in Princeton. Noticing the darkening sky, he turned to his assistant.

"Guess it's going to storm, Jim," he said.

Jim nodded and continued his work. A little rain was nothing to worry about.

A minute later the tornado hit. Phillips was lifted, along with most of his office furniture, and deposited outside in a mud puddle. Terrified, Phillips lay in the puddle, holding his arms over his head, until the whirling winds subsided. Then he looked up cautiously, surprised that he was still alive. Slowly he rose to his feet and glanced around. His office was a mass of rubble. Two automobiles had been blown away. Then he saw a movement in a coal pile and realized it was Jim, digging his way out.

Glad to be alive, the two men walked back to their demolished office. Phillips remembered that there had been a thousand dollars in bills in the cash drawer. The cash drawer and bills were gone.

Four miners were enroute home from work by automobile when the rotating funnel swooped down on them. The tornado swept the car away, but not before it carefully plucked the four men from the auto and transplanted them safely at the side of the road.

A quick-thinking seventeen-year-old persuaded his mother and two brothers to lie down on the floor of their house beneath a rug. All were saved from injury when the roof blew off the house and showered the rug with glass and debris.

E. F. Shine, an engineer on the Southern Railroad, was near Princeton when the twister veered toward the tracks and headed directly for his train. Funnel and train collided; the train was the loser. The cab of the engine was torn off above Shine's head, but he held on tightly and gunned the train through the whirling funnel. He escaped with only a few scratches.

People were protected by their homes or killed in them. One man saved himself by crawling under the kitchen table, where he escaped being crushed by falling timbers when his roof collapsed. A woman was blown against her own fireplace and killed.

Griffin, a village of 400, was totally destroyed. The town was flattened by the tornado and then burned. Of 200 buildings in the city, only 4 remained standing, and these were badly mauled. Fifty people were killed and almost 200 injured.

Oddities of the storm were plentiful. Fire raged through one small town because the fire engine itself was burned to a crisp. A mine clerk took refuge inside his office safe; it protected him from crumbling walls and flames. A family crawled under an automobile, which sheltered them as the walls of their house tumbled over the car. A letter with a Poseyville, Indiana, postmark, was found in Bloomfield, 100 miles away. An Illinois Central Railroad bridge shifted six feet from its concrete pillars. A grain elevator was picked up and neatly set down in the middle of a road, 40 feet away. A rescue worker, noticing a baby's shoe protruding from the wreckage of a home, pulled on it and found there was a baby attached to it. The child was unhurt. The owner of a general store was hurrying home along some railroad tracks when the tornado dipped toward him. He clung to the tracks, suffering a broken shoulder, arm, ribs, and fracture of his spine, but he never let go.

An inspector for a lumber company was eating in a restaurant when the tornado tore the place apart. "The roof went off first," he said later, "and then all four sides were swept away. I was left sitting there with nothing around me. Then I left."

By the time the tornado finished with Indiana, its force had nearly been spent. One small spin-off from the tornado caused property damage and casualties in Kentucky and

Tennessee, but the Tri-State Tornado was finished. It rose, never to descend again.

The day after the tornado, a *New York Times* reporter flew over the devastated area and wrote one of the most graphic accounts of the destruction:

> Below is a little city, [it reads] impotent after this, the latest lesson on the weakness of humans. The airplane is just finishing a tour of a large part of the district devastated late yesterday afternoon. From the vantage point of the air it is painfully easy to trace the serpentine course of the demon of the winds. Like a huge boa constrictor, it winds its way over the three commonwealths, crushing all in its path.
>
> Houses are few and rare. Suddenly appears a vacant space, where it is apparent a house should be. There is a barn with a few cows huddled near for warmth, and there is a boxed hedge, lining what was once the entrance walk to a fine, solid American home.
>
> There is a cellar, we find. One can see the potatoes and other products for home still in their neat barreled rows, but there is not a semblance of a home, not even a scrap of torn timbering. And in front of this fallen hearthstone, this instant crushing of the toil of a lifetime, an old man and a woman stand and gaze vacantly into the pit. No, their arms are not around each other. Steadfast even in defeat, as the fictionists would have it, they stand apart, bent and gray, so hopeless that neither can add to the other's burden by a touch of tears.
>
> Five miles speed fast when the airways roar. There in the long trail we find the answer to the mystery behind us. For more than a mile this Illinois farmer's home has been laid down, a piece here, a timber there, like jackstraws lengthened out.

Swooping over Princeton, the writer says, "One quarter of it has been destroyed. We come down closer. A huge factory has had its roof and insides sucked out by the wind. Another plant, apparently a railroad car-shop, has been wrecked. Hundreds out of work, probably, to add to the burden of woe. And, as we find later, twenty-one bodies are beneath the rows of white sheets.

"In Princeton, as elsewhere, are the same numb groups of twos and threes on every street corner. The same silent throng in front of the *Clarion* office, reading the bulletins, and in front of the morgue, waiting for another body to be brought from the shattered heaps in the ravaged area."

In the wake of the tornado, uncovering bodies and rescuing the injured were grim occupations for every town struck by the disaster. It was slow, heartbreaking work, and when it was done there still was a monstrous cleanup job—and finally the rebuilding of each community, almost from scratch. But aid poured into the three devastated states. Within five hours, rescue workers were scrambling over the tangled heaps of debris. The American Red Cross sent much-needed supplies and rescue workers from St. Louis. Chicago offered a half million dollars and the Illinois Legislature appropriated a like amount. Money, clothing, food, and medical supplies arrived from across the country. Doctors labored long hours to help the injured.

Mass funerals were held in the stricken towns, and afterward survivors who had lost relatives and friends to the tornado buried their grief and returned to the difficult task of rehabilitation. Many did not know it then, but the 1925 Tri-State Tornado was the worst single twister ever to attack any area of the United States. It claimed more lives and did more damage than any other tornado since 1884, when a series of tornadoes swept through the southern states, killing 600. In only four tornadoes since 1884 has loss of life reached 500. The Tri-State Tornado killed 689.

An unnecessary act of cruelty added to the deep grief of tornado survivors in Griffin. A few days after the tornado ripped through town, a religious service was held for survivors. Most of the people in the congregation had lost loved ones—a father, mother, child or close friend. They sat, waiting numbly for whatever solace the minister could give.

They received, instead, a mournful castigation by the Reverend Harold M. Cordell, captain of the Evansville group of the Volunteers of America. He said that "God visited affliction on the wicked," and that it was as an atonement for wickedness that the tornado wiped Griffin off the map, killing more than 50 persons and injuring many others.

If the tiny village of Griffin had ever been a sin-town, nobody was aware of it, and the simple, hard-working men and women listened in shocked silence to the accusations. There must have been anger and outrage among them, for they countered the minister's condemnations in the only way they could. When the preacher asked them to join him in a closing hymn, nobody sang.

13

The Palm Sunday Tornadoes
Midwest, U.S.A. (1965)

It was Palm Sunday, April 11, 1965. Throughout the Midwest the weather was warm and balmy. City dwellers took advantage of the coming of spring to perform the perennial task of taking down storm windows and putting up screens. Farmers prepared their fields for spring planting. Those seeking relaxation crowded the golf courses and picnic grounds, and a few sun worshipers tried to pick up an early tan.

It was a perfect day for such activities, but it was also a perfect day for tornadoes. Weather bureaus throughout the Midwest were aware of this fact, and they issued warnings that heavy thunderstorms were in the offing and that a tornado was possible.

A tornado, indeed!

What actually occured on that lazy afternoon and well into the evening was not one tornado but a series of them, an epidemic of twisters. There were so many, striking out in every direction, that it was impossible to keep an accurate count. But the figure that survives is 45—almost half-a-hundred vicious twisters that battered more than 50 towns and communities in the states of Indiana, Iowa, Ohio, Illinois, Michigan and Wisconsin. The multiple attack from the air lasted ten horrendous hours, killed 271 people, injured more than 5,000, and left countless numbers homeless. Property damage was estimated at $200,000,000.

Residents of the six ravaged states had become so accustomed to tornado warnings that they paid little attention to them. The only people seemingly worried about a possible catastrophe were the meteorologists at the Severe Local Storms Forecasting Center in Kansas City, Missouri. Conditions were ripe for tragedy. A single large squall line had developed over the Texas-Oklahoma area, as dry polar air from the northwest overrode moist warm air moving up from the Gulf of Mexico. This ominous line of thunderstorms, capable of spawning tornadoes, was moving northeast.

Two unusual factors concerned the weather watchers. One was the speed with which the storm moved. Instead of the normal 35 miles an hour, it was forging ahead at a 46-mile-an-hour clip. The other factor was an extremely intense jet stream racing west to east over the top at an altitude of six to eight miles—a flowing river of air that would worsen the storm below.

At 1:20 P.M. the first funnel was sighted south of Dubuque, in eastern Iowa. Within an hour, six more were reported in Iowa, Wisconsin and Illinois. Two of these sideswiped Watertown and Monroe, two small Wisconsin villages, demolishing several buildings and killing three people. The thunderstorm line that formed the base for the tornadoes cut off electrical service to 350,000 people in the area.

But that was only the beginning. By three o'clock the blackened line of thunderstorms was hovering west of Chicago, and the weathermen in that city noted that the line stretched from De Kalb, Illinois, to Madison, Wisconsin—a distance of 100 miles. The storm was apparently headed around the lower tip of Lake Michigan where it would then cross into Indiana, Ohio and Michigan.

At 3:15, Chicago weather watchers spotted an ominous sight—not one but a large colony of funnel clouds doing a macabre dance as they moved in a northeasterly direction. They were dipping down to touch the ground with their deadly tips, bouncing wildly into the air again, then descending once more like lethal daggers aimed at the earth. From that time on, more and more funnel clouds were reported, traveling in a variety of directions, bouncing along in crazy, unpredictable patterns.

There was, literally, no place to hide.

Illinois was the first state to feel the brunt of the multiple tornadoes. In the northern part of the state, twisters struck towns at random. Three suburbs of Chicago—Geneva, Mundelein, and St. Charles—were hit, causing no deaths but injuring scores. Near Rockford the Wagon Wheel Motel was damaged, and north of that city a farmhouse was leveled. At Island Lake some 50 houses were knocked down by a twister that killed an eight-year-old boy and injured at least thirty-five. The same twister destroyed a hanger sheltering ten airplanes, leaving one twin-engine plane smashed to bits.

Although Chicago itself was not hit by a twister, heavy winds blew signs off of two buildings, killing a child and injuring four, and a seventy-mile-an-hour gust blew off a hangar door at O'Hare Airport and turned three KC-tankers around ninety degrees.

But Crystal Lake, northeast of Chicago, became the hardest hit community in Illinois. Out of a black sky a twister descended on a residential neighborhood lying just outside the business district. Roaring out of an open field, it bounced across a highway, leveled a gas station, smashed the Crystal Lake Plaza Shopping Center, uprooted trees, tore the roofs off houses, caved in walls and impaled a rowboat on the limb of a tree. The twister rose, then touched down in another residential section, repeating its pattern of destruction. In the two sections of the town hit by the tornado, at least 100 homes were destroyed. Six people were killed and a large number suffered serious injury.

A sequence of bizarre occurrences accompanied the devastation at Crystal Lake. Charles Swanson was taking a shower, getting ready to attend a christening party. As the angry twister roared down on his house, walls and ceilings collapsed all around him, and Swanson was sucked out of the shower stall. "The next thing I knew," he said afterward, "I was sliding out into the street with no clothes on. I got up and there was no house left and I could hear my wife hollering from the basement that she was all right but couldn't get out." A quick-thinking neighbor rushed to Swanson's aid with a pair of pants, and then the two men began to dig through the debris that had once been the Swanson home until they freed his wife.

Mrs. James Berning was watching the storm from a window of her home and noticed a television antenna fly by like a kite. As she stared in amazement, a driverless automobile rolled into her front yard—then the roof of her house sailed away.

Charles Oberlin sent his family to the basement when he realized a tornado was rampaging through the city, but before he could follow them he was pinned against his living room wall. The twister held him there until it passed over. The wall Oberlin had been blown against was the only one in the house left standing.

Having dealt Illinois its savage blows, the barrage of tornadoes moved into Indiana. Here they actually struck twice—two series of twisters sweeping over the state three hours apart—and the death toll and destruction were far worse than in Illinois. Entire families died as their homes caved in on them. Motorists were killed when their cars were swept from the road. Crumbling buildings buried victims in rubble. Downed telephone poles and trees blocked highways and streets, sometimes crushing people as they fell.

Just before the onslaught, Elkhart County Sheriff Woody Caton heard the weather bureau warn of approaching tornadoes. Looking out the window of his Goshen, Indiana home, he saw a black funnel that seemed to be heading directly for a nearby trailer park. Caton got into his car and headed for the park, arriving just after the twister had carved a path of devastation through the compound.

Caton was appalled at the sight that met his eyes. Almost a hundred trailers had been flattened. A dozen were standing on end. Trailers had been torn from their frames and twisted into pretzel-like shapes. Trees and power lines were down; paved walkways were buckled. Bodies were strewn around the park, and bloodied survivors walked about in shock.

Caton quickly commandeered the help of the uninjured and began the work of freeing people trapped in debris. As they labored, another funnel loomed on the horizon and began to approach the park. "It looked as if it was coming right at us," Caton said later. "It was very big. It didn't have that kind of corkscrew-type spiral. This one looked like the stem of the ugliest mushroom I'd ever want to see."

Fortunately the twister shifted course, and Caton leaped into his car and followed it. Two miles away the tornado dropped down on a residential section. When Caton arrived, the scene duplicated that at the trailer park. Houses were down, bodies lay on the ground, and the injured stood mute, looking at the shattered neighborhood that had once been home. Said Caton, "Trees were twisted and twisted again and then ripped in half. The tornado scared the paint off of cars, squeezed them together like accordions, or exploded them as if by dynamite."

Scores of small towns lay in the paths of scores of twisters. At Lebanon the ugly black tongue of a twister lapped up seventy-five homes like a greedy monster, killing seven people and injuring many more. In Dunlap a tornado demolished a trailer camp, turning mobile homes into tangled wreckage, killing 20 residents and injuring 91. Eight-month-old James Petro, Jr. was luckier than most. He was lifted from the crib in which he slept, transported 175 feet by the winds, and deposited gently in an open field. All the child suffered was a black eye.

Marion received trip-hammer blows from three successive tornadoes. Bargain hunters in a shopping center were buried in debris as the twisters wrecked buildings, and many elderly patients at the Veterans Administration Hospital were treated for shock after one of the tornadoes blew the roof off.

Kokomo was another ravaged community. The tornado that bounced into town demolished the Holiday Inn, sending at least a hundred people rushing from the dining room as the building collapsed. The west wall of the Chrysler Transmission Plant was torn off and fifteen workers were injured. An apartment complex was leveled, resulting in many deaths and injuries.

Three churches in Russiaville were destroyed in identical fashion: In each case the congregation huddled in the basement while the church itself was blown away above their heads. A bank in the town was blown down, except for one wall—the wall with the safe in it.

After their orgy of destruction in Indiana, the mass of tornadoes broke in two—one bundle heading east into northern Ohio, the other northeast into Michigan. The major Ohio city battered by a tornado was Toledo, close to the Michigan border. The murderous rotating wind descended on the city at 9:30 P.M., when darkness made it impossible for people to see its approach. It hit a northern suburb of Toledo called Fuller's Creekside, where it slaughtered 15 people, injured 200, flattened 25 homes and severly damaged 35 others. The violent destruction was accomplished in a few terrifying minutes.

Most people were caught totally unprepared. Leo Baranski and his wife were watching television in their home in the Toledo suburb when the program was interrupted by a warning of possible tornadoes in the Michigan area. Mrs. Baranski turned to her husband, relief in her voice, and said, "Honey, aren't we lucky that the tornadoes are going to miss us?"

Before her husband could reply their house crumbled around them.

Eighteen-year-old Valerie Canney, alone at home with her dog, Penny, had little advance warning of the tornado's approach—but she had some. Penny's agitated barking awakened her and she heard a rumbling noise. When Valerie saw the walls buckling, she quickly crawled beneath some heavy furniture. The house collapsed, but the furniture protected her from injury. Her panic-stricken parents, arriving home within a few minutes, found the girl unhurt, but the bed she had been sleeping on was discovered a half block away. The heroic little dog was killed.

Gene Cerveny told a story of horror and heroism. His home was badly damaged by a twister, but Cerveny managed to escape into the open. A neighbor's house had completely disappeared, and Cerveny approached the hole where it had been. "I saw a father and mother and four children huddled in the corner of the basement," he related afterward. "They had nothing over their heads but the sky. It was horrible."

Next Cerveny saw the Reverend William Jones, pastor of the Lutheran Church, standing in the middle of the street, dazed. He was wearing a T-shirt and shorts and blood was seeping from several wounds he had suffered. The distraught minister said, "I've lost my whole family!"

Cerveny rushed back into what was left of his own house to get dry clothing for the minister. Then the two men started toward the Jones home. On the way they pulled several people from rubble, and when they reached the minister's battered house they were able to rescue his wife and family from the debris—still alive. Two people who had been visiting the minister were dead, however.

The Toledo-Detroit Highway near the state line was a scene of chaos and death. A Short Way bus had been flipped over on its back by the whirling action of a tornado, killing two passengers and the driver. Four huge tractor-trailer trucks were blown off the freeway and several cars were over-turned.

Traver Watkins, his wife and three children, were return-ing to Michigan from a vacation when the twister hit them just south of the Ohio-Michigan line. "We were driving under a viaduct when I saw it coming," Watkins said. "My wife, Lucille, shouted for me to back up the car. I reversed it but it still rolled ahead. All at once this thing picked up the car."

The entire family was thrown from the automobile, and Watkins spent anxious moments slogging through a muddy field before finding his wife and children. His wife and one child were injured.

Two truck drivers, Arnold Cook and Albert Alter, miracu-lously escaped harm when their vehicles were toppled near the Watkins car. "We knew," Cook said later, "that there was a bad storm and that a tornado had been expected. But I'm sure I heard a radio report that the danger had passed. It hadn't—not for us, anyway. I saw Al's truck flip in the wind. Then it was me—up in the air and over on the side. It was quite an experience."

In Michigan's nearby "Lost Peninsula," a tiny spit of land that juts into Maumee Bay just north of Ohio, a twister lev-eled twenty-three homes and killed two women. In a freak occurrence, the rotating winds picked up a thirty-five-foot cabin cruiser in the bay and dropped it on top of a house; it smashed through the second story of the home and came to rest in the living room. Another trick of the wind sucked up an automobile and dumped it upside-down a block away. It was found later with a rocking chair, swaying gently in the breeze, perched on its understructure.

Michigan was battered by tornadoes that dipped down from the blackened sky to wreak havoc on towns and farmlands throughout the southern half of the state. In addition to the individual tornadoes, cyclonic winds cut a 200-mile-long path across Michigan's southern counties.

Tragic incidents abounded in the paths of what one weather forecaster called "a family of tornadoes." Eighty-three-year-old Esterline Short went to the door of her trailer home ten miles south of Grand Rapids to view the storm. A tornado hit, plucked her from the doorway and tossed her aside like a rag doll. Then it picked up the trailer and carried it away. In a camp near Kalamazoo, thirteen people were hurt when every trailer in the park was tipped over. North of Lansing a tornado picked off five homes and two barns and reduced them to rubble within a minute. In Owosso two fire station roofs were blown off. At Reading a father and three young children were swallowed up by a tornado and tossed 100 yards from their home; two of the children were killed.

A sixteen-mile stretch of Branch County near the city of Coldwater had double trouble. The area was hit by a tornado at 7:15 P.M. and then struck by a second twister a half hour later. The two tornadoes followed the same path, the second one destroying what the first one missed. Branch County Sheriff Keith Wilheim said, "The first one had us reeling. The second knocked us out."

Two resort areas on Coldwater Lake—Pearl Beach and Crystal Beach— were demolished by the twin twisters. Fortunately, most of the cottages in these two sections were unoccupied. Sheriff Wilheim said, "The toll of injured and dead would have been terrible two months from now."

Many people who narrowly escaped the first twister were caught by the second. Juel Weigh, a Branch County deputy, was dispatched to the stricken area after the first tornado hit.

As he neared Coldwater Lake, his car was caught by the second tornado. The whirling winds plucked him from his vehicle, rolled him along the ground for 75 feet and left him tangled in the branches of a fallen tree. His car was destroyed. Erwin Feller, a lakeside resident, stepped outside after the first tornado had passed to inspect the damage done to his guest house. While he was so occupied the second came along and destroyed his home. George Ivey was in his resort home with his wife, son, and three grandchildren. "We heard this roar," he said. "Then my garage came slamming through the house." Mrs. Lucille Strang took an unscheduled ride in her trailer when the first tornado tossed it 50 feet into the lake. Mrs. Strang was pulled to safety by neighbors.

After the twisters passed, hundreds of residents in the area were taken to a Coldwater hospital for treatment. Among them were two victims of unusual injuries: a man with wood splinters driven deeply into his hip, and a woman with a four-inch piece of straw imbedded like an arrow in her neck.

Something of a miracle took place just north of Grand Rapids at a bar and grill where 75 people were having dinner. Among them was eighteen-year-old Fred Smoes, who gave an account of the total destruction of the restaurant:

> There was this rumble, like a freight train [he said] and quite a few people ran to the front of the restaurant to see what was happening. Then things started crashing and everybody hit the floor—almost as if by instinct.
>
> There was some screaming and a few people were cut, but no one was seriously hurt—and that's a miracle. Windows crashed, parts of the front wall collapsed, bottles sailed around and a portion of the top of the building just flew away somewhere. I didn't stop to think whether it was a tornado or anything else—I just fell to the floor.

Smoes remained under a table for about five minutes and, when the disaster seemed over, he got up and started to explore the devastation. "Everybody was wet and dirty," he said. "We walked around and saw that across the street houses were flattened. All power and telephone lines were out. There were a lot of cars in the parking lot next to the restaurant that were smashed and there was a semi-truck on its side."

Smoes was impressed by the fact that nobody in the restaurant was killed, but he was even more astounded at a sight he saw across the road. Right in the middle of the wreckage of several houses an elderly woman sat quietly in an easy chair. "I guess everything around her must have been carried away while she was in the chair," he said.

In Kent County, north of Grand Rapids, a fusillade of funnels wreaked havoc. The raging twisters ripped through rich fruit lands and laid waste to a two-mile strip of Alpine Road, running north from Grand Rapids. Along the road, Frank Ingersoll, a 70-year-old farmer, and his wife were tending to chores in their barn when they heard what sounded like low, muttering thunder and the fall of hail. Instinctively they headed toward a corner of the barn just as a portion of the roof collapsed. Hay poured down, almost burying them. When the tornado faded into the distance, they emerged unhurt. But they found that the house they had lived in for 26 years was gone. Nearby, William Oiree and his wife tried to reach the basement of their home as the twister roared down, but they didn't quite make it. The house collapsed, two cars in the couple's garage were blown into a field, and a child's tricycle was impaled on a tree limb. The Oirees were both injured. Mr. and Mrs. John Ostrowski and their children were out of town when the tornado tore through the area, but they returned to heartbreaking destruction. The small home in which they had been living while Ostrowski was building a new house was wrecked, and the home he had spent five years working on had disappeared. "I'm so grateful the children were out of the house that I'm ashamed to even cry,"

Mrs. Ostrowski said later. "But when I think of all the work my husband did on the new house, I just can't help it."

The list of destruction seemed endless. Here a roof was torn off a home, there a barn was leveled. In one place all the trees of a 65-acre fruit orchard were torn up. A newly built church was demolished and a school flattened. Gravestones in a cemetery were scattered around like poker chips. A giant stand of pines was stripped of branches. Electrical towers of Consumers Power Company were toppled. The tornado had ripped through a golf course, destroying the pro shop and scattering golf clubs over the fairways and greens; scorecards belonging to the club were found as far as four miles away.

Robert Cordosa, aged 20, had a hair-raising ride in his car—through the air. "I was just a block-and-a-half away from home when I noticed the wind was coming up," he explained. "Then—whoosh—it took hold. The car was spinning around and I saw the top of a telephone pole. I thought it was coming toward me. Then I realized I was approaching it. I looked down and saw the top of a building, and just then the building disintegrated—like a dynamite explosion."

Cordosa went on to explain that his car hit the top of the telephone pole and sheared off. Finally the car descended to earth again and Cordosa crawled out of the wreckage. "The car looked like an accordion," he said. When the shocked young man stumbled home, his father took him at once to the hospital, but all he had were a few minor bruises.

In and around Manitou Beach, located near the Michigan-Ohio line, the death toll and damage was frightful. Slamming its way through the resort village, a twister struck a church packed with 50 people attending a Palm Sunday evening service, destroyed another church a short distance away which was empty at the time, flattened a $100,000 dance pavilion, and destroyed more than a hundred homes and cottages.

Lyle Ferguson, his wife, daughter, son-in-law and their two small children were attending a family reunion at the Ferguson farm near Manitou Beach when a twister raged through. It ripped the frame house apart and scattered pieces over a field, tore up three automobiles, flattened the barn, smashed several tractors, hurled a half-ton grain trailer against a tree—and killed all six members of the family in a split second. Nearby, Pearly Poling, a farmer, rushed his wife into the basement of their home as the tornado approached. Then, instead of taking cover himself, he set off across the fields to warn his son and daughter-in-law, who lived a short distance away. Poling never made it. An uprooted apple tree pinned him to the ground, dead. Meanwhile his son and daughter-in-law died in the wreckage of the house Poling was trying to reach.

The Reverend Jack Nicholson was at the pulpit of the new $75,000 Manitou Beach Bible Church delivering a sermon to half a hundred people when high winds began to shake the walls of the building. One of the worshipers, Mrs. Orin Brandish, later described the moment of terror. "Just before eight P.M. we heard hailstones rattling down," she said. "Some of the men went outside to look. Then the high winds seemed to die down, but suddenly there came a sound like a locomotive engine. Somebody yelled, 'Everyone to the basement!' Some people got downstairs but there wasn't enough time for all of us to make it. All of a sudden the building just seemed to explode in all directions."

The church crumbled under the fierce rotating winds of the tornado and Mrs. Brandish wound up unconscious, draped over a portion of one wall that still stood. When she came to, she noticed that she was covered with bruises and cuts and had been blown out of her shoes.

"Then I heard the most terrible sound," she said. "There were groans and cries of the injured and the screams of the children and people pinned in the wreckage, begging for help." Surprisingly, no one was killed, although virtually every member of the congregation was injured, some of them seriously.

Mrs. Robert Cunningham and her nine-month-old daughter, Linda, were in their home when they first became aware of a terrible storm approaching. "When I heard hail striking and the lights began to flicker," Mrs. Cunningham said, "I put my baby in her stroller and banked it with pillows in the middle of the living room. I went to close the kitchen door when the tornado seemed to blow right through the house. It picked Linda right out of the stroller and dropped her in front of me. Her head was resting on a window frame which had blown out. She was covered with debris and silent for a second or two. Then she began to cry. It was the most welcome sound I have ever heard. She had not been hurt at all."

Although the Cunningham home was badly damaged, the Cunninghams and the baby were unharmed.

When daylight returned to the stricken countryside of the six states pummeled by tornadoes, the extent of the damage became appallingly clear. The Palm Sunday Tornadoes—at least 45 in number—had whipped across the land, vanished in the upper air, and descended again an endless number of times, mercilessly battering houses and people with whirlpool winds measuring 300 miles-an-hour. So thick was the cluster of twisters that they stand today among the most destructive multiple tornadoes ever to ravage the midwestern United States.

Postlude

Many other natural disasters have been inflicted upon the United States and the Caribbean over the years. In any selection of such catastrophes, it is inevitable that some be passed over. The calamities described in this volume are those that seemed to me to have something special about them. They either are the most destructive, the most famous, the most dramatic—or simply, the most interesting.

Still, there are some other natural disasters that should not go unmentioned. Few great earthquakes have occurred in this country, other than the three covered in this book, but, in 1933, Long Beach, California, was rocked by a quake that killed 115, and Southern California was shaken in 1971, leaving 65 people dead.

Innumerable hurricanes have ravaged the eastern and southern coastlines of the United States. Those that claimed more than 100 lives include: Florida-Alabama, 1926, with 372 deaths; North Carolina to New England, 1944, with 389;

eastern United States and Haiti (Hazel), 1954, with 347; eastern United States (Diane), 1955, with 400; Mississippi-Louisiana (Camille), 1969, with 258; and Florida to New York (Agnes), 1972, with 117.

Volcanic action in this country and the West Indies has been infrequent. The eruption of Mont Pelee and the destruction of St. Pierre on Martinique stands out as the most devastating of all, but about the same time a volcano called Mont Soufriere on the British colony of St. Vincent erupted, spewing lava across one end of the island. It caused many deaths but nothing to compare with the toll at St. Pierre. Hawaii's Mauna Loa and Kilauea erupt periodically but rarely do much damage or claim many lives.

Floods, especially in the Mississippi and Ohio valleys, have been frequent, the most noted being the Ohio-Indiana flood of 1913 that claimed 732 lives, the Mississippi River flood of 1927 that killed 214, and the flood of 1937, when the Ohio and Mississippi rivers overflowed their banks and took 250 lives.

Blizzards occur mostly in the northern sections of the United States, but the only blizzard other than the 1888 storm described in this book that took more than 100 lives occurred in the same area in 1958, with 171 dead.

The South and Midwest have experienced more tornadoes than it is possible to list. Some of the worst include: Alabama, 1932, with 268 deaths; Tupelo, Mississippi, 1936, with 216; Gainesville, Georgia, 1936, with 203; and Arkansas-Missouri-Tennessee, 1952, with 208.

Man has learned lessons from such disasters. He can take certain steps to protect himself. But he has never learned how to prevent natural catastrophes, nor has he found any way to minimize them. If the description of the foregoing natural calamities illustrates anything, it is simply this: When nature decides to war on mankind, she has all the weapons.